"With eloquence and grace, Isaac V[...] [...] ity, heartbreak, and resilience foun[...] [...] Mexico borderlands. Embodied in these stories of spiritual communion—from Tijuana to Durham, NC—is a profound treatise on hope, struggle, and the power of solidarity across borders."

—FELIPE HINOJOSA
John and Nancy Jackson Endowed Chair in Latin America and Professor of History, Baylor University; author of *Apostles of Change: Latino Radical Politics, Church Occupations, and the Fight to Save the Barrio*

"With this book, Isaac Villegas has taught me how to think theologically about migration and how to think alongside migration about God. In so doing, he has transformed my understanding of Christian spirituality and of the practices that constitute Christian life."

—LAUREN WINNER
associate professor of Christian spirituality, Duke Divinity School; author of *The Dangers of Christian Practice: On Wayward Gifts, Characteristic Damage, and Sin*

"The Christian story remembers the plight of migrant people who believe and hope in a migrant God. Isaac Villegas offers us testimonies to inspire our politics and argues that our action must begin with worship and prayer. This is a book for our times."

—MARÍA CLARA BINGEMER
professor of theology, Pontifical Catholic University of Rio de Janeiro, Brazil; author of *Latin American Theology: Roots and Branches*

"Isaac Villegas's *Migrant God* isn't just a book full of powerful, often overwhelming, stories. It is certainly that. But it is also a book that serves as a powerful, often overwhelming, political 'vision of belonging'—reminding us that amidst the darkness of what nations do daily to God's migrant people, a light overwhelms the darkness, and the darkness has neither overcome nor comprehended it."

—JONATHAN TRAN
associate dean for faculty and associate professor of theology in Great Texts, Baylor University; author of *Asian Americans and the Spirit of Racial Capitalism*

MIGRANT GOD

—

A CHRISTIAN VISION
FOR IMMIGRANT JUSTICE

—

ISAAC SAMUEL VILLEGAS

WILLIAM B. EERDMANS PUBLISHING COMPANY
GRAND RAPIDS, MICHIGAN

Wm. B. Eerdmans Publishing Co.
2006 44th Street SE, Grand Rapids, MI 49508
www.eerdmans.com

Book design by Lydia Hall

Printed in the United States of America

31 30 29 28 27 26 25   2 3 4 5 6 7

ISBN 978-0-8028-8443-5

Library of Congress Cataloging-in-Publication Data

A catalog record for this book is available from the Library
of Congress.

Biblical quotations are from the New Revised Standard Version,
unless otherwise noted.

CONTENTS

INTRODUCTION

During a weeklong stay at a shelter in Tijuana, Mexico, I picked up a book of prayers for migrants: *Una luz en el camino* (*A Light on the Journey*). The book is published by the Scalabrini order of priests who've established houses for migrants along the routes up through Central America into Mexico, and finally to the border with the United States. People from across the Americas, and across the world, shelter with them in Tijuana for a few weeks, sometimes months, while preparing to cross the desert into the United States. Others are there to recover from the grief of failed hope—for the quest, the struggle to come to a sudden end on the other side, *al otro lado*, at the hands of border police. The trauma of capture, detainment, and deportation. Their American dreams turned into nightmares.

The Scalabrini prayer book offers words as balm for the duress of migration, to comfort people who suffer the harsh realities of the border. "En ti, oh Dios, depositamos afanes y desvelos" (We entrust our toils and sleeplessness to you, O God). "En silencio ante ti, seguros, descansamos" (We rest secure in the quiet of your presence). "Tu paz es nuestra dicha" (Your peace is our blessing). "Nos ponemos confiados en tus manos" (We put ourselves, with confidence, in your hands). These are lines from early in the book, a psalm about our confidence in God: "En Dios ponemos la confianza."[1]

Here, in my home in North Carolina, I've been praying through the collection as I reach for spiritual links to the people I've met—people with whom I've shared fellowship as they've prepared to cross the border, as well as friends on this side who've suffered the incessant fear of deportation. These prayers help me to sustain a spiritual connection, as part of my political solidarity, with neighbors near and far who persevere in the tribulations of the borderlands. With the prayers I bind my faith to theirs in a communion of words.

Those prayers enliven my book—words of supplication for safety while on the move, for comfort while living through nightmares, for peace while walking through valleys overshadowed by death. Words to sustain hope in God's promises. The chapters in this book invite you to share in both my lament at our harmful politics and my hope for our transformation. To love our neighbors with the love of Jesus is at the heart of Christian ethics. To pray for neighbors on this side and the other side of the border is to lift up their lives before God, and to consider how God might answer their prayers through our solidarity, through our love, which is an expression of our devotion to the God of life. We make their concerns our own because we are each other's keeper. Every person is a child of God, which means all of us are siblings. When one of us suffers, all of us suffer. When one rejoices, we all rejoice.

The theme of this book is my relentless hope for God's redemption, personally and politically, in our churches and our society. These pages are prayers for heaven to transfigure the earth. Prayers of repentance from our collective harms, and healing for our political woundedness. We've fashioned communities on a global scale that are inhospitable to people who've had to leave their homeland. Nation-states develop immigration policies and implement enforcement strategies as fortifications against people trying to survive, fellow members of the human community doing what we as a species have always done: moving from region to region for a better life, seeking refuge in the aftermath of crises, the human pursuit of social well-being.

In her 2016 article for the *London Review of Books* about the refugee crisis in the Mediterranean Sea, historian Frances Stonor Saunders writes about our deadly world: "I don't understand the mechanisms by which globalisation, with all its hype of mobility and the collapse of distance and terrain, has instead delivered a world of barricades and partition."[2] I haven't been able to shake from my memory her account of over five hundred Eritrean and Somali asylum seekers on an overcrowded boat that capsized between Tunisia and Sicily.

They reached the coastal waters of the Italian island of Lampedusa. "Among the 108 people trapped inside the bow was an Eritrean woman, thought to be about twenty years old, who had given birth as she drowned."[3] Saunders describes the horrific scene. "Rescue divers found the dead infant, still attached by the umbilical cord, in her leggings."[4] For the rest of the article, Saunders recounts her investigation into the whereabouts of this woman and her child. "I do want her to be known by more than just the number she was given after being hauled out of the water—288 (and 289 for her baby)."[5] She tracks down a journalist who interviewed the partner of the young, dead mother. He survived and now, heartbroken, has had to figure out how to go on without them. His partner's name was Yohanna, he said. Saunders concludes her account with a crushing sentence: "In Eritrean, [Yohanna] means 'congratulations.'"[6] Her death was a drowning of hope, the death of hopeful expectation. Her and her family's dreams ended with a nightmare.

The International Organization for Migration has documented 3,129 migrants either dead or missing in the Mediterranean in 2023, and more than 30,000 since 2014.[7] For most of them, we will never know their names. But loved ones somewhere know, and remember. To honor the people who've drowned off their shore, the residents of Lampedusa include memorials in their cemetery—plaques with the words "Unidentified Migrant."

I don't have firsthand experiences of the terrors in the Mediterranean. I only know of the situation there from others' accounts as I try to keep track of international immigration politics and the global plight of people who risk their lives for safety, for a good life somewhere. This book is not an analysis of our situation worldwide. Instead, I focus on what I've experienced and the people I've met while engaged in our collective struggles for immigrant justice here in my American homeland. I was born in Los Angeles, California, to a Costa Rican mother and a Colombian father. I grew up in Tucson, Arizona, in the US borderlands, and I have lived in Durham, North Carolina, for most of my adulthood. My life, my family, my belonging reaches across three American countries. In these pages, I draw on the resources available to me—biblical and theological, spiritual and political—to describe what I've witnessed of immigrants and nonimmigrants who have lived out their hope for a country where citizens and noncitizens can belong together. My reflections have to do with my own life, my pastoral work, and immigrant justice organizing and activism. I don't engage in arguments to convince US citizens to change their minds about our neighbors who haven't been able to obtain legal permission to justify their lives in our country. Those books are readily available. Mine, instead, assembles—from what I've glimpsed in our struggles and solidarities—a piecemeal vision for a people transformed through dedication to the work of collective wholeness.

This hope is alive. I've seen this vision made flesh in communities along the US-Mexico border (for example, in Tijuana, Mexico, and Douglas, Arizona—see chapters 1 and 3) and far away from the borderlands (for example, in North Carolina—see chapters 5 and 6). In these pages I tell the stories of ordinary people—with and without US citizenship—who profess their devotion to each other through their steadfast love. According to the theologian Dorothee Sölle in her book *The Mystery of Death*, we express Christian love in our solidarities, in the companionship of our love as we struggle for the safety and well-being of all. "The best translation of what the early Christians called *agapē* is still 'solidarity.'"[8] My book, I hope, bears witness to the perseverance of this kind of solidarity, as people demonstrate their love in the streets and through hospitality in migrant shelters (see chapters 3, 4, and 5), in their endurance in detention centers and their mutual care in cooking meals (see chapters 1 and 3).

I dedicate this book to two people: Rosa del Carmen Ortez-Cruz and Samuel Oliver-Bruno. Both of them became part of my life through our church's participation in a solidarity network of sanctuary congregations in North Carolina. I spent a lot of time with Rosa over the past several years when she lived on church property in our attempt to keep her safe from threats of deportation. I'm still in awe of her perseverance, her existential commitment. Every day for two years she would wake up and decide to stay in the protective care of our church as the courts processed her immigration case—all for the sake of a future here, in the United States, with her children. She lived her faith in God's strength. I'm still astonished at her trust in our church's promise that we would keep her safe for as long as she needed. While I've recited countless times that line from the Apostles' Creed about believing in the church ("I believe . . . in the holy catholic church"), Rosa has taught me the existential meaning of that confession. To believe in the church with her life, to entrust herself to a congregation—she has lived her hope in the people of God to offer the provision of the Spirit. Chapter 6 recounts Rosa's story of sanctuary.

As for Samuel, the last time I saw him was inside the Wake County jail in Raleigh, North Carolina. He was in a cell across from mine. Plainclothes officers had tackled him to the ground, taking him by surprise, arresting him at the US Citizenship and Immigration Services (USCIS) office where he had been summoned for a biometric appointment. During the Trump administration, Samuel's work permit had been unexpectedly rescinded, and he was ordered to self-deport—to leave behind his life and responsibilities here in the United States and remake himself in Mexico, the country where he was born. Instead of abandoning his wife and son, Samuel lived with his family under the protective care of a Methodist church in Durham as part of the sanctuary movement: a network of congregations, including mine, that had welcomed undocumented residents to live on church property where Immigration and Customs Enforcement (ICE) agents had been ordered not to trespass. He lived at the church while trying to apply for legal permission to stay. When he ventured out of the church building to the USCIS office to fulfill a requirement for his application, despite promises that he wouldn't be taken into custody, a squad of ICE agents abducted him from the waiting room. People from his church, along with members of our extended sanctuary community who were there to provide accompaniment, dashed around to the back of the building. They crowded around the ICE van where the agents had taken Samuel. Friends blocked the vehicle from driving away and texted alerts for others to converge upon the office building. I rushed to the scene as soon as I heard the news.

By the time I arrived, a hundred people had gathered in the parking lot. I made my way through the crowd to the circle of friends and strangers who had surrounded the van. Through the tinted windows I could see Samuel in handcuffs in the back seat. I locked my arms with the others, adding my body to our human chain, a wall of almost thirty people encircling the vehicle—our last-ditch effort to keep him with us. After an hour-long standoff, the local police chief heeded the call from ICE to remove us. Twenty-seven of us refused to leave Samuel. We remained at the van, side by side, until police officers pulled our arms apart to handcuff and arrest us. They transported our group in a caravan of vehicles to the jail, the same one where Samuel would be incarcerated as the first step of his deportation.

Inside the jail, after officers had processed and escorted us to holding cells, we saw Samuel across a corridor—and he saw us. He lifted his hand to his heart and bowed his head toward us. The officers took him away, deeper into the recesses of the facility. In the early morning, before daybreak, ICE agents drove him to Stewart Detention Center in Georgia. Within days, he was deported—released in Matamoros, Mexico, across the border from Brownsville, Texas. In 2021, still separated from his wife and son here in North Carolina, Samuel died in Mexico.[9]

The title of this book, *Migrant God*, refers to both the God who migrates and the God who is in solidarity with people who migrate—the God who, in the tabernacle, joined the biblical people of Israel on their pilgrimage in the wilderness. "And have them make me a sanctuary, so that I may dwell among them," God directed Moses on how to organize a movable home for God's presence with the liberated Hebrews after their enslavement in Egypt (Exod. 25:8). As the people wandered in the desert, God wandered with them. The tabernacle was a sanctuary for the divine presence at the center of their encampments. This same God became human in Jesus—the incarnation was a divine act of solidarity, for God to join our plight. "And the Word became flesh and lived among us" (John 1:14). The Greek word for the verb "lived" in that verse is from the root *skēnoō*, which means "to tabernacle." In Jesus, God has tabernacled with us, just like God's wilderness sanctuary with the Hebrews. The Spirit of God dwells with people on the move. A migrant God for migrant peoples.[10]

- 1 -

DEATH IN THE DESERT

In the town of Douglas, Arizona, in the municipal cemetery next to the US border wall, I noticed clusters of cement blocks lodged in the sand with the same word etched into their flat surfaces: Unidentified. "Unidentified Female," "Unidentified Male," carved into the center of the tablet, along with a date—"Found Aug. 9, 2004," "Found Dec. 31, 2005," "Found Jan. 18, 2009," "Found Feb. 12, 2009." In a hushed tone, speaking over my shoulder, a Mennonite activist explained that the date marks when the remains were found in the borderland wilderness—a corpse in decomposition, a skeleton bleached in the sun, perhaps only a skull or a set of teeth.

A few of the older grave markers had "Unknown" instead of "Unidentified." Local immigrant advocates petitioned for the change to "Unidentified" because while they did not know the story of the human remains, they did know that each person had a family, that every one of them was a parent's child, someone's friend. The gravestones remember people who were beloved, known and loved by family members now desperate for information, longing for an explanation, waiting for a phone call, searching official lists for the name of their loved one. Every unidentified life was known.

I was there in the cemetery to join pastors and humanitarian workers for a prayer service. We huddled in a circle among the graves and joined our voices in a petition for God to comfort all who longed for the return of their lost ones. "We light this candle as a sign," we said in unison as the votive passed from hand to hand, "that we hold in our memory the lives of our sisters and brothers who have died in the desert." The last person with the candle placed it on the ground at the center of our circle. In the quietness, we watched the slender flame flicker in the breeze. Then one of the organizers invited us to sing along with her, to let the lyrics guide us into hope.

> Peace is flowing like a river,
> flowing out of you and me,
> flowing out into the desert,
> setting all the captives free.

The words focused my gaze on the wall beyond the cemetery, the barricade at the border, and I begged the sky for monsoon storms to rend the heavens with apocalyptic rains—a primordial deluge, flash floods gushing through arroyos, pounding against the metal barrier, bending steel and devouring concrete with a fierce torrent of destruction.

The weather's intervention in our border politics had happened before. "A 40-foot stretch of mesh border fence east of Lukeville in Southwestern Arizona," Brady McCombs of the *Arizona Daily Star* reported in 2011, "was knocked over Sunday by rainwater rushing through a wash."[1] The water cleansed the landscape. The environment ravaged the blockades at the border. The earth reminded the government of ancient passageways. Nature frequently devours our structures of violence that have been built into the wilderness. I sang my prayer for peace flowing like a river—but peace as a cataclysmic flood, a disaster for the US Border Patrol's infrastructure, peace as a movement of nature to set migrants free.

Through an interlocking system of fences and walls and surveillance outposts, the United States has implemented a border enforcement plan as part of a tactical war in the desert. Francisco Cantú, a former US Border Patrol officer, outlined this sinister strategy. "Our policy of prevention through deterrence—pushing those crossing out from the heavily patrolled urban areas to the remote areas of the desert—serves to weaponize the landscape," he said in a 2018 interview with *Vox*. "That's why people are dying in the desert."[2] US agents scavenge the borderlands, hunting for water outposts set up by humanitarian organizations. When they discover these oases—covered by mesquite and paloverde trees, hidden among the creosote bushes—Border Patrol personnel gouge the canisters, emptying the water into the sand. As Cantú writes in *The Line Becomes a River: Dispatches from the Border*, "It's true that we slash their bottles and drain their water into the dry earth, that we dump their backpacks and pile their food and clothes to be crushed and pissed on and stepped over, strewn across the desert and set ablaze."[3] From 2012 to 2015, Tucson-based La Coalición de Derechos Humanos and No More Deaths found that "at least 3,586 gallon jugs of water were destroyed in an approximately 800-square-mile desert corridor near Arivaca, Arizona."[4]

The architects of this war against migration have built a deadly environment. According to their 1994 national strategy report, the US Border Patrol outlined a plan to redirect migrants into the most dangerous regions of the borderlands: a "shift in flow," with the results that "illegal traffic will be deterred, or forced over more hostile terrain."[5] They have, indeed, succeeded. "The government chose to funnel people through the desert areas, and it created a killing field," Isabel Garcia, co-chair of La Coalición de Derechos Humanos, explained to the Sierra Club in 2018.[6] "Over the last two decades," La Coalición de Derechos Humanos and No More Deaths report, "the remains of at least 7,000 people have been recovered in the United States borderlands."[7] Premeditated death, the result of strategic planning.

The desert wilderness has become "a landscape of death since the 1990s," Joseph Nevins argues in *Operation Gatekeeper and Beyond: The War on "Illegals" and the Remaking of the U.S.-Mexico Boundary.* "U.S. authorities are arguably responsible (at least partially) for the deaths by knowingly 'forcing' people to take death-defying risks."[8] Our government's prevention through deterrence policy allows us to lie about the border, to obscure the effects of our politics. The policy provides our society with plausible deniability for the gruesome scenes in the wilderness. The infrastructure of the built environment redirects migrant trails into the harshest of terrain in order to shield us from our culpability. We can shrug and look away. Life is tragic, we tell ourselves. It is what it is. We prefer not to know, which is the purpose of the 1994 enforcement strategy—for us to become a people who don't have to consider the human costs for our way of life. These losses are the result of the militarized occupation along our border with Mexico, Nevin argues: "The land and its peoples are very much under occupation—literally and figuratively. The presence in the borderlands of thousands of heavily armed state agents and various barriers and military-like technologies are just the most visible manifestations."[9] In my own lifetime, I've witnessed the drastic escalation of militarized vehicles on patrol in southern Arizona, as well as the military installations and fortifications along the border—as if that federal border strategy launched in the 1990s were a plan for a slow escalation in an all-out war.

According to the UN's International Organization of Migration, 686 people died or disappeared in 2022 while crossing into the United States through the desert, "making it the deadliest land route for migrants worldwide on record."[10] In a 2022 investigation, the US Government Accountability Office discovered that the Border Patrol has failed in their responsibility to keep track of the number of migrant deaths: "Border Patrol hasn't collected or recorded complete data on migrant deaths and does not have a plan to evaluate how [their] program is working."[11] These lives, apparently, aren't even worth a number in a federal database. The migrant dead, forgotten by the state. Disappeared.

But even the disappeared leave traces. In response to the crisis in the borderlands, Robin Reineke became involved in the work of identifying remains and locating next of kin in order to let them know about their loved ones. She cofounded the Colibrí Center for Human Rights in Tucson for these purposes and is now a sociocultural anthropologist at the University of Arizona. "When one sees these remains in person, it is very hard to see them as anything other than the result of violence," she recounts in her chapter for *The Border and Its Bodies*. "What I have seen is blackened skin stretched thinly around bone. I have seen bodies without faces, without arms, without feet. I have seen mummified remains where the skin is as hard as leather. I have seen the teeth marks of animals. I have seen bones that are bleached, gnawed on, dismembered, or crumbling."[12]

The deadliest region of the Sonoran Desert on the US side of the border is part of the Tohono O'odham nation, whose citizens bear the repercussions of legislation not of their making, a violence not of their design. Their land soaks up the death instigated by US policies. Reineke tells the story of her encounter with a Tohono O'odham man who was tending to the violence in the desert. She had joined the annual Migrant Trail Walk, a weeklong pilgrimage in desolate regions of Arizona, in which participants carry crosses with the names of the dead in order to honor their memory. One day late in the week, in an area south of Tucson, the group of pilgrims saw two people in the distance beside a truck parked along the road that cut through the bleak landscape: "a Tohono O'odham man and his young son were waiting for us." She continues with her account:

> The man was carrying a staff adorned with red ribbons and small cloth pouches. He explained that he had traveled all the way from the western reservation that day to greet us and to thank us for honoring the dead. He wanted his son to see that there were those who cared. He had brought a sacred staff and tobacco that had been blessed. He told our group, "We used to clean the earth each time we found a dead body. Now, we find so many dead that we don't even know how to clean the earth anymore. It hurts us, and it hurts the land."[13]

The Tohono O'odham are healers whom I'itoi, their divine creator, has entrusted to restore health to the community, an ecosystem that includes human beings. Harms against migrants are an affliction that spreads across the created order, a bodily violence that is a spiritual wound bleeding into the landscape.

Baboquivari Peak overlooks that anguished stretch of the borderlands—sacred lands, imbued with a holiness that holds all creatures together in a relationship, a wholeness shared among soils and trees, cacti and birds, rocks and humans. In the O'odham language, Waw Giwulk is the name of the mountain range, known as the navel of the world, the birthplace of all peoples. I'itoi still lives there and watches over all who journey through the labyrinth of life and death.[14]

Mike Wilson, a Tohono O'odham member, has also watched out for people who cross the border into the wilderness under I'itoi's care. He has maintained water stations near the town of Sells, the capital of his nation. "The Tohono O'odham people have a tradition of hospitality. They've always offered humanitarian aid to migrants," Wilson explained to a reporter with the *Phoenix New Times*. "But 500 migrants coming across the reservation on a given day has exhausted this tradition of hospitality."[15] Despite the overwhelming demands of neighborliness, of care for people in distress, in existential crisis, he has persevered with his humanitarian aid, in his routines of refilling canisters and leaving jugs of water along migrant trails through tribal lands.[16]

In the early chapters of Genesis, Cain kills his brother, Abel, and abandons his remains in the wilderness outside the gates of the Garden of Eden. Cain returns to normal life as if his brother's disappearance will go unnoticed, as if the world will forget Abel. But God keeps vigil and confronts Cain. "Where is your brother?" God asks. "I do not know; am I my brother's keeper?" Cain responds, masking his culpability. "Listen," God calls out, "your brother's blood is crying out to me from the ground" (Gen. 4:8-11).

This story has haunted me as I've walked through the borderlands, wondering about lost siblings, listening for their blood crying out from the sand—sisters and brothers from beyond the border who didn't make it. Kindred from across the Americas, dead and gone before I could welcome them as neighbors. These deaths are like that first murder. Immigration policies and border enforcement strategies have deafened us to the blood. We are like Cain.

A whole landscape of anonymous skeletons and mass graves, untold horrors—the dead are victims of enforcement mechanisms that conceal personal responsibility. Indirect murder. Killing without pulling a trigger. In *Migra! A History of the U.S. Border Patrol*, Kelly Lytle Hernández—professor of history, African American studies, and urban planning at the University of California, Los Angeles—tracks how officials have always included the environment's weaponization within their enforcement plans as a way to absolve border agents from blame. In the 1950s, "immigration law-enforcement techniques shifted responsibility for the number of deaths associated with undocumented immigration to migrants themselves."[17] By erecting border fencing and consolidating agents in urban centers, US enforcement strategists deputized the landscape. Agents kept their hands clean while heatstroke and dehydration did the dirty work. They could absolve themselves of the blood. "The Border Patrol had relocated the danger of immigration law enforcement to the natural landscape of the borderlands," Hernández notes. "Migrants battled deserts and rivers rather than men with guns."[18]

US agents didn't need to give an account for the deaths. No one had to claim responsibility for the remains. "When bodies shriveled in the desert or washed up on the banks of the Rio Grande, no one could be named in the death of the migrants," Hernández writes. "Fingerprints could not be dusted from the sand, and the rapids left no tracks to be followed."[19] They converted the stark beauty of sand and rivers and mountains into "a system of violence without perpetrators"—anonymous killers, murderers shielding themselves from liability behind reams of internal memos. "As a country coroner declared over the dead bodies of five migrants who had attempted to cross through the Imperial Valley desert, 'No marks of violence were found [on] any of the five bodies.'"[20]

As the death toll has mounted over the decades, US officials have continued to defend the strategy. Doris Meissner, the former Commissioner of the Immigration and Naturalization Service, remarked in the late 1990s, "We did believe geography would be an ally."[21] Or perhaps an accomplice—nature as an accessory to crimes against migrants.

Later that day in Douglas, in the McDonald's parking lot along the Pan American Avenue, I met up with several people from an organization called Healing Our Borders. Every Tuesday evening for over twenty years, this group has been hosting a vigil to remember migrants who've died in the desert. The first gathering happened on December 10, 2000, as a community response to the growing number of corpses found in remote regions of Sulphur Springs Valley, where the twin cities of Agua Prieta and Douglas are located, a community divided by a massive border wall of steel slats.

I was there with my friend Carol Rose, a pastor at Shalom Mennonite Fellowship in Tucson, Arizona. She arranged for a group of us to rendezvous with Jack and Linda Knox, two Mennonite retirees who had relocated to a neighborhood in Doug-las—a stone's throw from the border wall—to run a hospitality house as a hub for immigration justice work.

As we got out of our car, the Knoxes welcomed and recruited us to help unload crosses from their truck. We stacked them in a shopping cart, which Linda pushed to where the group had gath-ered in a shaded corner of the parking lot. Soon we hushed our conversations and Jack offered the official welcome for all thirty of us. He briefly recounted the story of the vigil's origins, locating the ritual in this local twenty-year tradition. He pointed to the cart filled with a hundred white crosses, each with the name of a person who was found dead in the Sonoran Desert surrounding the cities. The ones with us that evening, he said, were some of the 313 crosses that he and Linda keep at their house. When a body is found, another crucifix is nailed together, another name painted. If the coroner's office cannot determine a person's iden-tity, Jack added, the crosses are marked with the words "no iden-tificado" or "no identificada."

We began our procession at dusk. A friar invited us to take several crosses in our hands and follow the seasoned partici-pants. I grabbed three of them and followed the lead of an older woman. I walked behind her, all of us in single file, down the sidewalk of Pan American Avenue, a half-mile walk to the Raul Hector Castro port of entry, the border crossing station with Agua Prieta on the other side of the massive fence stretching from horizon to horizon.

I saw the first person at the front read out a name as he lifted a cross above his head, and everyone responded in unison, with a shout, "Presente!" He bent his body toward the ground to place the base of the crucifix in the street, at the edge of the pavement, leaning it upright against the curb on display for the passengers of cars on their way to and from Mexico. After this bow of reverence, he stepped out of the way and walked slowly to the back of our procession, awaiting his next turn. The second person in line, now at the front, called out another name and placed one more cross several yards further down the sidewalk. We processed like a dirge, our crosses as memorials, the avenue hallowed with our lament.

"Araceli Estrada Lopez y niño," I heard a woman call out the words written on her cross. A flash of horror trembled my body as I imagined a mother and her child lost in the desert, their remains in decomposition. "Presente," my voice wavered as I watched her lay down the cross.

As my turn approached, I memorized the names in my hands: Juan Tovar Hernández, Rosalía Ana Lilia Ramos Reyes, and Lucina López de Olmos. The woman ahead of me reached the front of our procession. She stopped, so we all waited for her shout. "No identificada," she called out with her crucifix shot toward the sky. "Presente!" we replied. She made her way to the back, picking up a couple more crosses from the cart that Linda pushed down the sidewalk alongside the procession. I glanced over my shoulder at the crosses along the curb behind us, remembrances for the dead in our wake, the named and unnamed people lost to the wilderness.

We veered from the walkway into a clearing before the kiosks where US officers check identity documents to determine who may pass legally across the border. Our group formed a circle for the closing ritual. Mark Adams, a Presbyterian minister who has helped organize the vigils from the beginning, took three crosses from the shopping cart. He stepped into the center and read aloud the name from one of them. All of us responded, "Presente!" He called out the next name. We replied, "Presente!" The last of the three didn't have a name, only the words "no identificado." Adams lifted the crucifix and shouted into the night, "Jesucristo!"—four times, facing east, then north, then west, then south, bearing witness to the corners of the earth. And each time we answered, "Presente!" Adams joined our circle as we linked hands and silenced ourselves in honor of the dead. In the middle, on the ground, the three crosses declared the area another Golgotha, with the militarized border as the crucifer.

After the vigil we wandered back along the sidewalk, gathering the crosses—one by one, name after name—and returned them to Linda's cart. The night shrouded our return, except for the cars' piercing headlights, which flashed across the glossy paint of the crucifixes that we'd yet to collect. The names flickered the lives of strangers into my mind, my last fleeting acknowledgment of the presence of their absence.

"Los pueblos crucificados." Crucified people. That was the phrase Ignacio Ellacuría used for describing the political and economic violences during the late twentieth century throughout Latin America, but especially in his community in war-torn El Salvador—the oppressed masses as crucified communities, a people devastated by the repression of a US-sponsored regime.[22] Ellacuría was assassinated in 1989 for his priestly work on behalf of disempowered and exploited campesinos. His fellow priest and colleague Jon Sobrino escaped the military assassination and went on, indebted to his martyred friends, to develop further the connection between Jesus's cross and the structures of violence that torment societies: "The cross of Jesus points us to the crosses that exist today.... The crucified peoples of the Third World are today the great theological setting, the locus, in which to understand the cross of Jesus."[23]

The crucified world of Ellacuría and Sobrino is also here, on this side of the border, as US imperialism throughout the Americas turns in on itself—not only with the desert as another Golgotha, but also with the social death that happens to undocumented people locked away in detention centers, like the one I've visited in Eloy, Arizona.[24]

Over a century ago, according to a local legend, when the train stopped at a desert outpost between Tucson and Yuma, a conductor new to the route looked out at the desolate landscape and recited the words of the crucified Jesus: "Eloi, Eloi, lema sabachthani?" which means, "My God, My God, why have you forsaken me?" (Mark 15:34). After that, the story goes, the derelict spot came to be known as Eloi, now Eloy, a city with a private prison to warehouse expendable people. Perhaps the legend was a prophecy, the train's conductor foretelling another Golgotha, CoreCivic's site for crucified lives.

The Eloy prison, a massive concrete edifice, loomed on the horizon—a stark, white structure jutting up from a patchwork of green cotton fields and brown desert soil. Layers of fencing enclosed the perimeter. I went there with a visitation group from Casa Mariposa Detention Visitation Program (now called Eloy Visitation & Accompaniment), an immigrant justice organization in Tucson. We turned into the compound where we saw a sign marking the entrance: "CoreCivic Eloy Detention Center, a Federal Contract Facility of the US Department of Homeland Security." The four of us piled out of the car and walked to the main entryway. An invisible hand clicked open the first gate with a loud buzz, allowing us to congregate in the intermediate enclosure. The gate shut behind us as cameras scrutinized our faces. After the visual inspection, the next gate opened, letting us into the facility. The guards checked our IDs as we passed through the metal detector, making our way to the waiting room. Women dressed in standard-issue prison uniforms emptied waste bins into their trash carts. A bulletin board on the wall indicated the current population of the detention center: 1405.

A guard escorted us through metal doors—sliding open in front of us, then locking behind us—to the visitation room where detainees sat in rows of plastic patio chairs. Some wore green clothes, others brown, a few blue—the colors indicating each person's level of privileges while incarcerated. All wore the same black shoes with Velcro straps. I sat in an open booth on the other side of the room, waiting for an officer to call out the names of the people on my list.

In the early nineteenth century, upon the arrival of the newly arrested at Auburn prison in New York, the warden would welcome the detainees with these words: "While confined here, you are to be literally buried from the world."[25] Prison is burial, an interment. "A living tomb," a prisoner named Harry Hawser wrote in a poem while incarcerated just up the road, in Philadelphia, at Eastern State Penitentiary.[26] When Charles Dickens visited Eastern State, he described the prisoner's experience as "a man buried alive, . . . dead to everything but torturing anxieties and horrible despair."[27] In more recent history, fifty years ago, George Jackson wrote a letter from San Quentin State Prison in California. "Capture, imprisonment, is the closest to being dead that one is likely to experience in this life," he said. "My life here is slowly becoming one of complete alienation."[28] Prison as alienation from life—that was his experience, buried behind layers of concrete and metal and bricks, behind walls and bars and fences. The contemporary poet Jimmy Santiago Baca, writing from the Arizona State Prison not far from Eloy, said that his time in prison felt as if he was confined in "an archaic tomb of concrete and iron."[29] Imprisonment is a labyrinthine passageway into the realm of social death: alienation from kinship, from community, from life. Migrant detention centers, as a feature of the US prison complex, deaden a person's humanity, estranging them from their sense of self. "Lo han dejado como a un Cristo," Ellacuría narrates life under the conditions of death's power—*to be abandoned as if another Christ.*[30]

At the Eloy facility, before our visitation time was over, I talked with one last person. He leapt to attention when the guard called out his name and pointed in my direction, smiling as he walked over. He shook my hand with both of his, exuding warmth and kindness. *Muy amable*, as we say. He asked about me, about where I was from, about my family, about work and hobbies. When I mentioned that I grew up in California, his face lit up. "That's where I grew up! In Fresno!" We exchanged stories about our home state. He was born elsewhere, but his parents brought him to California as a child. "Man, I miss that place," he closed his eyes. "I've been locked up for three years." I responded with shock. I didn't know that ICE detained people for that long in Eloy. "I mean, not just here," he said. "They've been moving me from prison to prison. Months here, then there, and everywhere because I get in trouble so they transfer me." He explained that he has multiple mental health diagnoses, and no one gives him the meds he needs, which means he suffers an episode of one sort or another and loses control.

"Since I've been in Eloy, three people have killed themselves in here," he shifted our conversation. "I don't blame them, 'cause the guards make our lives miserable. They're always messing with us."[31] I shook my head, glancing at the ceiling, then looking at him again. "I'm sorry, that's wrong," I said. "How do you do it?" I asked. "How do you get through the days and weeks

and months and years?" He grinned. "You gotta make up special
things, *hermano*, stuff to look forward to." He told me about the
previous week, about Christmas Day. "For *navidad* do you make
tamales?" he asked. "Of course!" I responded. "We make Costa
Rican tamales with banana leaves. How about you? You make
the ones with corn husks, Mexican-style, right?" He beamed with
pride. "On the outside, yes, *claro que sí*, with corn husks—the
right way, *hermano*," he winked. "But in here, you can imagine,
we've got nothing, so we get creative." He leaned toward me,
grinning again, and began to recount what he and his friends do
to celebrate Christmas.

"For months we save up the money that our people on the
outside send us, then we blow it all on stuff to make tamales, in
time for Nochebuena." They bought packs of Doritos from the
commissary, which they smashed into a chunky powder. "That's
what we use for flour." He described how he poured the pulver-
ized chips into a bowl and added water. "That's the masa." For
the filling, he explained, the commissary sells overpriced "pork
product." He rolled his eyes, "That shit doesn't taste like nothing, so we get some Tapatio and douse it." After careful assembly of Dorito masa and Tapatio-infused pork product, they took
a couple plastic trash bags and cut them into large rectangles.
"That's the only thing we could come up with for the husks," he
shrugged. "So we fold up each tamale in a strip of plastic, then
put them in the microwave for six minutes." I asked him how
much they'd spent. I could see him doing the math in his head.
"Eighty bucks for twelve tamales, but worth every dollar." In a
prison where guards administer misery to crush their spirits, that
Christmas meal tasted like a fleeting moment of freedom. "Just
talking about those tamales is making me daydream of next year
when we'll do it all over again."

I was the last one from our group to the parking lot. I hopped into the back seat across from Rocío Calderon, an organizer with Casa Mariposa. The two people in the front were already chatting. I stared out the window, watching saguaros and creosote bushes flash across the vista. After a while Rocío asked me if I was all right, if I wanted to talk about the visit. I stumbled over my words, trying to say that I didn't know what to do about such a hellish world, that nothing seemed like enough, that we needed to find a way to set everyone free from that torturous place, to end that existential nightmare. My response was a muddle of incoherence. Jumbled thoughts.

"I used to be there," she offered in an act of grace, letting me off the hook of having something to say. "Two years in that prison." She looked out her window. "Then Tina, a pastor of Shalom Mennonite in Tucson, visited me," she continued. "She came with the Mariposa group and somehow my name showed up on her visitation list." Rocío recounted how Pastor Tina had organized a group to raise money for bail. "I got lucky, for no reason, but there are so many others still there; there's no good reason why I'm free and they're not." She can't forget them; she won't forget. She writes letters to countless detainees and organizes others to write letters, Rocío told me. She gathers money to transfer to their commissary accounts. She coordinates visitation trips to the detention center. "We have to show them that they aren't alone in there, that they haven't been forgotten."

- 2 -

ANTIGONE AND ÁLVARO

At seven thirty in the morning I pulled into the Border-Links parking lot in South Tucson, the meetup spot for Álvaro Enciso's weekly pilgrimage into the desert wilderness with his crosses. The eight of us there loaded up the two Samaritan SUVs with jugs of water and headed down Interstate 19 toward Mexico. Our caravan took an exit west somewhere before Nogales—still twenty miles from the border. As we drove into the desolate landscape, a makeshift checkpoint suddenly appeared when we reached a bend in the road. A federal agent stopped us, plodded around our vehicles while peering through every window, then asked each of us if we were citizens.

We were twenty miles from the border, which is within what's known as "the Constitution-free zone" where the Border Patrol has been granted authorization to conduct warrantless searches and seizures, despite the protections of the Fourth Amendment. In her book *Illegal*, political scientist Elizabeth Cohen explains how the 1976 Supreme Court decision in *United States v.*

Martinez-Fuerte has empowered Customs and Border Protection (CBP) agents to "engage in acts that, for other law-enforcement officers, would be considered profiling."[1] This region now includes the majority of the people in our country. "Most of the US population—about two-thirds—lives in the official CBP border zone," Cohen points out, "that stretches around the entire physical boundary of the country, land and sea, and reaches into the interior one hundred miles at every point."[2]

With the checkpoint far behind us, we turned onto a dirt road that first followed along the property lines of cattle farms and then cut into a wilderness of mesquite groves and washes. The route took us up and down hills carved with gullies from season after season of monsoon downpours. The speedometer hovered at ten miles per hour for most of our journey deeper into the hinterlands of the Sonoran Desert, somewhere between Arivaca and Amado. Our guide was a handheld Garmin GPSMAP navigation device. We were on our way to where the remains of Lucio Sanchez-Zepeda had been found.

An organization called Humane Borders, in partnership with the medical examiner's office, hosts an online database that tracks deceased migrants. The website provides GPS coordinates for the spot where human remains were recovered. God only knows how many haven't been noticed, those who remain undocumented even after their death.

We pulled into a clearing and unloaded our supplies: a bag of cement, jugs of water, a shovel, and a cross. The next stage was on foot. Our single-file line snaked around creosote bushes and paloverdes. With the GPS device in her hand, the person at the front of our group led us to the place where Sanchez-Zepeda's remains were found a decade ago. The entry in the database noted that he most likely died of hypothermia.

We circled around the spot. One person dug; another poured the cement, then the water. Álvaro pushed his cross down into the hole, took several steps back, paused to look, then nodded to the rest of us. We gathered stones and placed them at the foot of the cross. "When you add a rock, you honor his memory," Álvaro told me. "You add your humanity, something of yourself, to this place."

To memorialize the dead is to claim a relation, to honor a mutual belonging, an intermingling—to recognize another's life as somehow part of our own. Álvaro marked the landscape with the sign of the cross to pay his respects and to include the memory of these dead in his life—to open a space within himself for them, for their plight and for the lives they could've had, but which were cut short.

"I came to this country in the 1960s because I was promised the American dream," Álvaro said, recounting his journey from Colombia to the United States as a young man. "Now, I'm out here to commemorate where dreams die, which is also a protest against the policies that kill our dreams and our lives." His word "our" claimed a kinship that transgresses borders, a transnational solidarity. To join him in the desert was to summon that kind of union, a spiritual communion as we linked our humanity to the lives of the dead through Álvaro's rituals of remembrance. The jug of water I carried from the SUV, the turn I took with the shovel, the rocks I added to the base of the crucifix—all were my contribution to his liturgical acts.

The word *liturgy* derives from the ancient Greek language: *leitourgia*, a compound term binding together *laos* (people) and *ergon* (work) to denote labor for a community. To work for the people—public service or public works for the common good.[3]

Our liturgy was for the community of the dead, to join our lives to theirs in an act of re-membering. In our ritual we declared our membership in a political body—like the ancient Greek polis— that refuses to live without a connection to the people who've died in the borderlands. With the crosses, Álvaro invited our participation in the care for the memory of the dead, to keep them from disappearing into oblivion.

These rituals of reverence cultivate a collective conscience as part of a political imagination that protests against the border. The crosses are signs of solidarity in defiance of our country's politics of alienation, in defiance of the violence involved in policing the division between citizen and alien. Our work was a kind of spiritual-political hospitality: to invite their spirits to occupy our minds and enlist our lives in the service of a stubborn hope for a world that doesn't yet exist, where no one will be sacrificed to protect the rights and privileges of citizenship. Álvaro's liturgies are prayers, prophecies for a polity that doesn't involve the blood sacrifice of migrants. Every crucifix planted in the wilderness is an act of devotion to a stranger who should have been our neighbor.

Beginning with Georg Wilhelm Friedrich Hegel's corpus in the early nineteenth century, Western political philosophy and political theology has turned to Sophocles's fifth-century BCE play *Antigone* to work through the conflicts of belonging and loyalties that emerge with the invention of the modern state.[4] The plot of *Antigone* circles around the scandalous burial of a person (Polynices) who had been excommunicated from the Greek polis of Thebes.

With their brother's corpse outside the city walls—Polynices's body banished as carrion—Antigone conspires with her sister, Is-

mene, to honor him with the rituals of burial despite the prohibi-
tion by Creon, their uncle and the ruler of Thebes.[5] "A city-wide
proclamation . . . forbids anyone to bury him, even mourn him,"
Antigone reports to Ismene. "He's to be left unwept, unburied,
a lovely treasure for birds to scan the field and feast."[6] The denial
of burial is punishment for Polynices's infraction, his attempt to
claim a turn on the family throne; Creon (his uncle) describes
his actions as a rebellion against their society, a revolt against
the order of the polis. In the drama, to honor the dead becomes
a political act against the sovereign's decree, a violation of his
law in order to extend the boundaries of the society, to include
the excluded.

Antigone refuses to abandon her brother's corpse to the
birds; she refuses to let her society discard the memory of his life.
She will not let Creon disappear the body. The rituals of burial
are her protest against Creon's efforts to banish Polynices from
eternal rest in the polis. To honor his remains according to the
customs of the gods is a declaration that his life, even after death,
belongs within a Theban political identity, included within their
collective self-understanding. She guards him from the birds,
from the oblivion of the sky, and instead entrusts him to the
land's care, for the earth to remember his life.

The dead have a claim on Antigone's life. "I have longer to
please the dead than please the living here," she tells her sister:
"In the kingdom down below I'll lie forever"—an eternal communion with the dead.[7] Ismene considers her sister's solidarity
with the dead to be insanity—beyond the reasonable behavior
befitting of citizens. "Why rush to extremes? It's madness, madness," Ismene says.[8]

But Antigone is obsessed. The death has affected her disposition, her personality. Creon describes Antigone's devotion as a

kind of hysteria: "You, with your eyes fixed on the ground."[9] Her posture toward the earth—her relationship to her slain brother's life poured into the soil—contrasts with Cain's repression of his murder of Abel in Genesis. "Where is your brother Abel?" God asks Cain. "I do not know," Cain responds, "am I my brother's keeper?" (Gen. 4:9). He denies responsibility for Abel's disappearance and disregards the bonds of kinship. Cain pleads ignorance and spurns God's assumption that he would care for the life of his brother. "Listen"—God turns to the earth, eyes and ears fixed on the ground—"your brother's blood is crying out to me from the ground!" (Gen. 4:10).

Antigone is nothing like Cain. Antigone is like God—both of them with heads tilted, bowed toward the site of the dead.

We're tempted to read from these stories about Antigone and God a categorical imperative to lament the loss of life—a prescription for a universal value to honor any and every death. In both cases, however, the narratives display an ethic far too partisan to reinforce that kind of laudable, humanist impulse. The God of the Bible takes sides in human conflicts: to accept Abel's sacrifice, not Cain's; to save Noah's family, not all the others; to choose Jacob, not Esau; to heed the Hebrews' indictment of Pharaoh's regime. The doctrine of election is the theological discourse we use to describe the partisanship of God. "God's election is . . . an election which genuinely divides," Swiss theologian Karl Barth explains in his *Church Dogmatics*.[10] He summarizes the arc of the biblical narrative as bending toward those who've been alienated from their societies: "The human righteousness required by God and established in obedience—the righteousness which according to Amos 5:24 should pour down as a mighty stream—has necessarily the character of a vindication of right in favour of the threatened innocent, the oppressed poor, widows, orphans and aliens. God always takes His stand unconditionally and passionately on this side and on this side alone: against the lofty and on behalf of the lowly; against those who already enjoy right and privilege and on behalf of those who are denied it and deprived of it."[11] God defends the defenseless and liberates the oppressed because that's the nature of God: a divine life in solidarity with people crushed in the gears of our politics. At the crucifixion of Jesus, this one who is God incarnate identifies with the crucified of our world. Christ crucified reveals the election of God, that God has decided to take sides, personally, existentially—a truth already revealed when God attends to the blood of Abel, a voice from the grave that testifies against Cain's violence.

Antigone also takes sides. As Bonnie Honig argues, "We find not a moralist humanist Antigone but rather a partisan political actor."[12] With a clandestine liturgy to honor Polynices's remains, she performs her devotion to a particular life—a rejected life. She dedicates herself to this allegiance, which involves a ritual of postmortem solidarity that puts her at odds with the politics of the sovereign. However, Antigone's act of reverence to the dead is not a universal protest against sovereignty as such, as if she desires a society without governance. She's not a proto-libertarian or an anarchist avant la lettre with anti-statist politics. Instead, Honig observes, Antigone "plots and conspires: she quests for power and seeks to infiltrate and claim sovereignty."[13] Antigone's funerary ritual and subsequent public grief invoke a hope for a community that wouldn't have severed Polynices from the body politic, during his life and after his death—a sovereignty reconfigured to include the one whom the sovereign, Creon, had cast out as an enemy of the polis. Antigone doesn't demand the destruction of Theban society; she instead summons her people into a different kind of social life. Her liturgy of mourning beckons a political vision that reincorporates the one whose corpse Creon left as carrion for the vultures.

In his testimony to Creon, a sentry recounts the grief Antigone had displayed as she buried the body: "She crie[s] out a sharp, piercing cry," he reports, "when she sees the corpse bare she bursts into a long, shattering wail and calls down withering curses on the heads of all who did the work." Oblations accompany her lamentation: "She scoops up dry dust, handfuls," the sentry narrates, "and lifting a fine bronze urn, lifting it high and pouring, she crowns the dead with three full libations."[14] Antigone's ritual of mourning is a political act of remembrance, a public liturgy to remember and rejoin the dead as part of the ongoing life of Thebes. Her lament, Honig notes, "takes sides" and demands "redress for a wrong." A politics emanates from her mourning, a partisanship that challenges the law and confronts fellow citizens with the collateral violence of their social arrangement, the framework of sovereignty that governs who belongs and who doesn't. "Our debt to Sophocles is his invitation," Honig writes of the ancient Greek tragedy, "to look hard at the myriad ways in which we silence the grief that in our politics we yet do so much to generate."[15]

Like Sophocles's tragedy, Álvaro's liturgies in the borderlands dramatize a refusal to acquiesce to the violence of our polis. His crosses locate the places where people breathed their last breath; his rituals hallow the ground where they gave up their spirits. He channels our sorrows into a demand for a politics without the collateral sacrifice of human life.

"You are a Mennonite priest, right?" Álvaro turned to me after we finished stacking rocks around his memorial for Sanchez-

Zepeda. "Here's holy water, if you want to sanctify the crucifix."
Last year a Franciscan friar joined the work of putting the crosses
in the desert, Álvaro told me, and he would sprinkle them with
his sanctified water. He gave the group containers of the water
to continue the practice after he left.

Álvaro handed me the plastic bottle, and I decided not to explain the differences between Roman Catholic priests and Mennonite pastors. I poured the hallowed water, which splashed on
the crucifix and rocks, then splotched the ground, soaking into
the caliche. "Lucio Sanchez-Zepeda, *presente*," I whispered, "the
Spirit of God, *presente*." At that cross, the place where a person
released his spirit with his last breath, to remember a life is part
of a liturgical politics of *epiclesis*—an invocation for God to make
these lives present to us, for the dead to be as present to us as the
resurrected spirit of the crucified Christ.

The Christian faith turns the living toward the dead. The torture and execution of Jesus Christ conditions our imagination,
our hope. Communion, a central ritual of the church, habituates
our posture toward the death of Jesus—and, through our memorial of his crucifixion, we bow our lives toward the victims of our
world's violence. The focus of the eucharistic words of institu-
tion, as passed on to us from the apostle Paul, is a death: "For as
often as you eat this bread and drink the cup, you proclaim the
Lord's death until he comes" (1 Cor. 11:26). The liturgy appeals
to his absent body; communicants re-present his life. Redemption, according to this Christian vision, is a stubborn memory.
Communion proclaims an eschatology in which the disappeared
aren't left behind.[16]

In the early centuries of the church, the faithful extended
this ritual in honor of Jesus to others who had died. Christians
gathered in cemeteries to share wine and bread with buried

corpses—a communion feast that included the dead.[17] The *Didascalia apostolorum*, a third-century treatise, offers counsel to those who, "in accordance with the Gospel and in accordance with the power of the Holy Spirit, gather in the cemeteries to read the Holy Scriptures . . . and offer an acceptable eucharist, the likeness of the royal body of Christ, both in your congregation and in your cemeteries."[18] To memorialize Jesus occasions the remembrance of other deaths. In the cemeteries, the eucharistic meal becomes a holy communion with the dead who are declared present with Christ. To proclaim the death of Jesus until he returns becomes a hope that has something to do with others who have perished. To gather for a ritual that remembers Jesus is a "dangerous tradition," writes theologian Johann Baptist Metz, the formation in a community of a "dangerous memory." The eucharistic liturgy, he explains, "claims unresolved conflicts that have been thrust into the background and unfulfilled hopes."[19]

In the borderlands, Álvaro's crosses are dangerous memories; they bear witness to the unresolved conflict of the border. Each crucifix remembers a life lost to the violence of immigration policies. His rituals gather a small community around unfulfilled hopes—to honor people who've journeyed across vast distances, who've persevered despite the unimaginable perils along the way, all for survival and for possibilities. Álvaro calls his work of remembrance "Donde Mueren los Sueños." His crosses mark the places where dreams have died, a landscape haunted with hope's expired breath.

On the long drive back to Tucson, Álvaro told me that he has installed a thousand crosses over the past decade. He assembles them in his studio at home, he explained, each one a work of art made with items found near other sites in the desert. "I use what people have had to leave behind, what they've dropped while on the run farther north." Photos from a wallet, metal from cans, canvas from backpacks, glass from bottles, rubber from a shoe. "Each of those objects marks part of someone's story, artifacts from a plot we'll never know," he said. "I include these fragments as a form of acknowledgment, of reverence, to honor them, for material from their lives to become relics on a cross."

He told me that the online database includes 3,600 deaths. "At this rate, four per week, I'll finish this work when I turn 127," he sighed. "But that doesn't even include the fact that more people die out here every week, every month, every year." He stared out the window for a while. "Let's just find a way to stop letting people die out here."

Back home, at my church, when I receive communion at the Lord's table—a piece of bread, a drink from the cup—I remember the broken bodies and the blood-soaked landscapes: the ground hallowed with Álvaro's crosses. At the communion table, the border draws near.

In *Antigone*, as incriminations circulate through the royal halls about who could have secretly performed the burial rituals for Polynices's remains in defiance of Creon's law, the leader of the chorus interrupts with his conjecture. "I've been debating in my mind," he says, "could this possibly be the work of the gods?"[20]

To honor the dead is holy work. Antigone and Álvaro offer divine liturgies, God's work.

HOLY MEALS, LAST SUPPERS

he Lord of hosts will make for all peoples a feast of rich food," Isaiah prophesied (Isa. 25:6). "This is the Lord for whom we have waited; let us be glad and rejoice in his salvation" (Isa. 25:9). When this biblical prophet describes life with God, he talks about a table with an abundance of food and drink. Salvation, Isaiah says, looks like a meal, an abundant feast, where people from everywhere fellowship together. Salvation is a heavenly banquet, a meal that tastes like heaven—with chairs crowded around a table, plates and bowls piled with food, and God as our host.

When I was a kid, when I'd visit my grandmother, *mi abuelita*, she always had *una olla* on the stove, boiling chicken for her *arroz con pollo*. I'd show up in the afternoon with my sister, and my grandma would spoon hefty portions of *arroz con pollo* into bowls for each of us. I'd return in the evening with my cousins, and she would serve us *arroz con pollo* before we went out for the night. At her house, when visitors would stop by, she'd insist that they sit down for a feast of *arroz con pollo*. If we'd stay long enough for dessert, she'd pass around *arroz con leche* with *pasas*. I learned the mysteries of the kitchen as I watched and helped.

"Mi casa es su casa," she'd say (My house is your house)—and her table was our table, where we found ourselves in her care, as part of her family, along with all the guests who were becoming family. Her table was a glimpse of "the kin-dom of God," as *mujerista* theologian Ada María Isasi-Díaz puts it. *La comunidad de fe* is *la familia de Dios* (the community of faith is the family of God) where we are all kin, all of us part of a *kin-dom*.[1] "For us Latinas," Isasi-Díaz explains, "salvation refers to having a relationship with God, a relationship that does not exist if we do not love our neighbor."[2] God's kin-dom is like my grandmother's home where there was always room around the kitchen table for another neighbor, another stranger, another guest—an expansive vision of kinship, of who is a member of a household. Salvation looks like my grandmother's table, where friends and strangers learn how to belong to one another, where we catch "eschatological glimpses, part of the unfolding of the kin-dom," Isasi-Díaz writes.[3]

To be together is the gift of salvation. To fellowship is a glimpse of the kin-dom of God. Isaiah's prophecy invites us into an experience of our world where salvation tastes like a communal meal, with God as the cook who has prepared a feast—a steaming pot of *arroz con pollo*—and a kitchen table with plenty of room. At meals, as we recognize ourselves at God's table, we eat and drink the goodness of God. We find ourselves at a feast where we receive each other's companionship as divine nourishment. God's table extends the household of God everywhere, adopting us into a kin-dom that doesn't recognize the border's attempt to segregate peoples. We learn the taste of salvation at meals, at feasts that feed our longing for God's hospitality to break open our worldly forms of inhospitality.

At the southeastern edge of Dallas, Texas, I showed up early for the worship service at Luz del Evangelio, a Mennonite congregation. The sanctuary was already packed with people who'd gathered for the pre-worship Bible study. The congregation, I discovered as I slipped into the back row, was making their way through the book of Esther one passage at a time, Sunday after Sunday. This week, the exegetical discussion turned into a passionate lesson, with pastor Juan Limones calling upon his flock to live as a community set apart for the work of the Holy Spirit. "Somos el pueblo de Dios," he explained. "Y porque somos el pueblo de Dios, vivimos de forma diferente en el mundo." As the *pueblo* of God, the church has a distinctive form of life, similar to Esther and her people in the Bible story. "Como Esther, tenemos costumbres diferentes—parecemos diferentes al mundo." He described church life as a kind of cultural formation that renders them different when compared to some of their worldly neighbors.

And, like Esther and her Jewish community, God's *pueblo* perseveres amid threats to their lives. Pastor Limones used the figure of Haman, the villain in Esther's story, to name political leaders and immigration enforcement agents who were taking away "los hermanos y hermanas del pueblo que no tienen papeles" (sisters and brothers without legal documentation). So, like Esther's community, "tenemos que orar" (we need to pray). The *pueblo* prays with confidence, "con fe," he continued, "porque tenemos Jesucristo, nuestro abogado en el cielo, a la diestra del Padre." Jesus Christ takes their side as a heavenly immigration attorney whom the Father has entrusted to defend the lives of the *pueblo*'s citizens. Christ is the advocate above every earthly authority—*el abogado en el cielo*—protecting the people of God.

To conclude the Bible study, Pastor Limones invited the crowd to the front of the sanctuary for intercession. With hands reaching up into heaven, congregants prayed aloud—a multitude of voices, a polyphony of tongues, supplications wafting like incense, like the scene in the book of Revelation where "the smoke of the incense, with the prayers of the saints, rose before God" (Rev. 8:3–5). In response, according to the Bible passage's revelation of spiritual realities, God will strike the worldly arrangements of oppression with lightning bolts of divine mercy and justice. "Fuego, fuego, fuego," Pastor Limones called to God, "el fuego del Espíritu Santo" (the fire of the Holy Spirit). "Santo, Santo, Santo," he prayed from the pulpit, "llénanos con tu presencia" (fill us with your presence).

The worship leader then joined the pastor on the stage and turned the prayers into an announcement of grace: "El Señor quiere un pueblo liberado" (the Lord desires a liberated pueblo). "Libre, libre, libre en ti, Jesucristo. Aleluya!" She proclaimed freedom, liberation, through Christ. "Somos libre en tu presencia." The worship team assembled behind her. Their music summoned the congregation to praise, each person with their own song. Some remained up front, others knelt at their chairs, and the rest of us stood with raised hands, offering our hearts and lives to God. Through her microphone, a singer on the stage added her voice to the melodies, "Levanto mi corazón, levanto mi vida!" The power of God thumped through our bodies with the rhythms of the drum. "Dios es poderoso!" shouted the worship leader (God is almighty!). Yet the all-powerful God was also a gentle presence. "En esta reunión Cristo está," the leader whispered into her microphone (Christ is here in our gathering).

"El presencia de Dios está aquí," she continued in the same quiet tone. There, in God's gentleness, children played on the floor and under the chairs while their parents sang of God's love—and all of this was praise.

Through a door at the back of the sanctuary, worship spilled into the kitchen. I wandered over to peek at the bustle. As the door swung open and closed, I glimpsed worshipers kneading *masa* for tortillas and crushing large watermelons into juice—liturgical food and drink, the preparations for our communal meal. After Pastor Limones's sermon, we gathered outside. We sat and stood around tables with a feast of tacos, tamales, and *jugo de sandía*. During the week of my visit, the worship services on Friday and Sunday ended with meals, with celebrations that extended a table from earth to heaven.

El pueblo de Dios is a kin-dom where we all belong, where salvation is a banquet of *arroz con pollo* and *jugo de sandía*.

Meals with others provide God's solace and strength, even when the table is set in the valley of the shadow of death, with the threat of enemies on the horizon.

In the darkness before dawn, from the top floor of La Casa del Migrante's housing complex in Tijuana, Mexico, I stared across the cityscape at the US border wall aglow in artificial light. Along the border, massive poles with clusters of industrial bulbs illuminated the dry river valley on the US side while casting the wall's shadow into Mexico. I was the first one up—just me and the neighborhood roosters. My morning responsibilities included the essential task of making sure the coffee was warm before the shelter's residents rushed to catch their buses for work.

I unlocked the kitchen and flipped on the lights. The cauldron rested on the gas burner. I had already mixed the instant granules into water and brewed the coffee the night before. Enough for the fifty adults in the compound, as well as the dozens of people from the streets who soon would be waiting at the gate for breakfast—*café y pan.*

While the vat of coffee warmed, I set out bread and cereal for the morning, then I pulled yesterday's leftovers from the walk-in refrigerator and started scooping food into containers for workers to take with them for lunch. Soon other volunteers made their way down to the kitchen in time for the steady stream of residents—first the people who depart early for jobs, then a couple hours later everyone else: parents with children and adults without work.

After the breakfast bustle, whoever was still around lingered in the open-air courtyard until staff arrived and gathered the kids for educational activities while the adults began their community chores.

La Casa del Migrante is part of the Missionaries of St. Charles–Scalabrini, a Roman Catholic religious order founded in 1887 to minister to migrants. Their shelter in Tijuana was established in 1987. Currently, the priests run four shelters in Mexico: Guadalajara, Nuevo Laredo, Tijuana, and Mexico City. Globally, the Scalabrini International Migration Network administers over 250 local ministries in thirty-three countries, all in service of people on the move: individuals and families who've fled from violence, from political oppression, from wrecked economies, and from the devastations of our climate crisis. The Constitutions of the Scalabrinian Congregation focuses the order's work on a "preferential option" for people who are "living the drama of migration."[4]

Fr. Pat moved from Latiné ministry within the Roman Catholic Archdiocese of Kansas City, Missouri, to Tijuana in 2013 when his order appointed him to serve as the director of La Casa. He has described the shelter as "a field hospital on the frontlines of immigration battles, a place of healing where people find an oasis of hope in the desert of deportation."[5] Over a quarter of a million people have sheltered there while heading north to cross the border or while picking up the pieces of their lives after deportation from the United States. "We strive to offer radical hospitality to those who enter our *casa*," Fr. Pat told me, "in the spirit of Jesus in Matthew's Gospel who tells his disciples to welcome strangers as if they were him."

Six long-term volunteers had kept the shelter operational during the COVID-19 pandemic. I was there for a week to help with the work and to provide some relief in the kitchen from the endless labor of cooking for the residents. While at La Casa I took the morning shift to give the others a chance for a few more hours of sleep, of rest from the daily grind of radical hospitality.

After the morning rush, Miguel, the community chef, walked into the kitchen, strapped a bib apron over his shoulders and around his waist, and began the prep work for dinner. I put away the last of the breakfast food, clearing space for his workstation, while he darted around the cooking area methodically organizing ingredients and kitchen utensils. He was making arrangements for his ingenious dinner plan for using the two turkeys the shelter had received the day before—his culinary brilliance focused on turning donated items into delicacies. "I like to make meals they can't afford," he explained, "because everyone should get a chance to delight in food."

While attending to the turkey preparations, Miguel instructed me in the art of making *arroz y frijoles* for a hundred. He gently scattered chunks of red onion into a massive pot of shimmering oil. I stirred with a wooden spoon the size of an oar as they blistered. "Para darle sabor," Miguel explained as he fished out the onions and set them aside for the turkeys.

He dumped a bucket of rice into the pot. The grains crackled in the oil. "The rice needs to brown but can't stick to the bottom," he said while showing me how to stir. Immediately, I got the spoon stuck in the clumps of rice. As I tried to work it free, I kept on banging the spoon against the metal rim. Miguel showed me the technique again, the rhythm of how to push and pull the rice. His work looked like a dance with the pot as his partner.

I lost track of time as I focused on the rice and tripped over my feet. After ten minutes, twenty minutes—at some point Miguel came over and poured a bucket of *caldo*, the leftover water from a chicken he had boiled the day before. As the rice simmered, he added another bucket, this one filled with the tomatoes and onions and garlic he had asked me to liquefy in the blender earlier that morning. Then, in the form of a cross, he sprinkled a handful of salt into the pot. I watched in silence and felt like I should also cross myself *en el nombre del Padre y del Hijo y del Espíritu Santo*.

There, in Miguel's kitchen, with both of us gathered around *una olla de arroz*, a scene about Heraclitus flashed to mind. Pilgrims were in search of the great philosopher of ancient Greece, and they found him in a kitchen near the stove. "Come in," Heraclitus invited them, "for there are gods here too."[6]

The morning shift, which began before daybreak, ended at two in the afternoon. In the shower I washed away the layers of cooking grease, then I rested for a while in the volunteer lounge on the fourth floor. Soon I heard the bustle of life from below and returned to the courtyard. I joined a long-term volunteer,

Anny from Costa Rica, as she served bowls of *jicama con tajin*, a pre-dinner snack.

In the kitchen, new arrivals to the shelter made Salvadoran guacamole, which, to the surprise of Anny and me, included hard-boiled eggs. A woman from Sinaloa, Mexico, rolled out her masa for tortillas—*de harina, hecho a mano*—and passed them to her son who fried them on *la plancha.* Moments later she squeezed a lime and sprinkled salt on the warm tortilla she had put in my hand. As we feasted on tortillas, she told me that her family fled from home a couple weeks ago after the cartel had tried to recruit her sixteen-year-old son. She, her husband, and her son were now on their way to her sister in Fresno, she said, if they could cross. "Pastor, ¿podrías orar por mí?"

Life at La Casa revolved around the kitchen—from before dawn until after bedtime. Someone was always there preparing for the next meal or cleaning up after the last. Around the stove, people shared their stories. We shared our lives.

After dinner, with the dishes cleaned and the floors mopped, Miguel passed me a beer and I asked about his favorite food to make. "Rice and beans, arroz y frijoles," he answered without a second thought, "porque nunca van a faltar." This kitchen comes with a huge responsibility, he explained, because so many depend on us for their food. "We cook to sustain the gift of life, as strength for the journey, como una bendición para los que tienen que cruzar."

Before his ascension, before the resurrected Jesus crossed from earth to heaven, before his disappearance—the joining of his life to the multitudes of the *desaparecidos*—he cooks a meal for his friends. One morning, at dawn, Jesus roasts fish and warms bread over a charcoal fire. "Come and have breakfast" (John 21:12). He serves the disciples after their long night of work at sea. "Jesus came and took the bread and gave it to them, and did the same with the fish" (John 21:13). Like my *abuelita*, he takes time to make food—to feed the hungry, to care for human life, to gather people into the kin-dom of God.

At La Casa every meal was holy: *café y pan, arroz y frijoles*. The domestic arts of the kitchen were sacred rites of communion—tortillas *hecho a mano* with a spoonful of Salvadoran guacamole. Food and stories passed from person to person—conversations about who had crossed yesterday and wonderings about who might cross tomorrow. Every meal was a last supper. I whispered prayers to myself for their safety, for no more broken bodies, no more deaths.

- 4 -

PROTEST AND PRAYER

n 2010, early in President Obama's administration, we began to hear heartbreaking stories from neighbors and friends. Fathers taken into custody at worksites. Mothers arrested at driver's license checkpoints. Members of our community disappeared at the hands of local police. In Zebulon, a town at the eastern outskirts of Raleigh, city and county police set up a checkpoint at the entrance to a Latiné immigrant congregation during worship services. Congregants at Iglesia de Dios, Catedral de Jesús reported that officers waved through white and Black drivers but stopped for questioning cars with brown people at the wheel.[1] In the cities of Apex, Cary, and Durham, agents raided construction sites. At the end of their two-day operation, they arrested and detained twenty people who were suspected of living in the United States without proper immigration papers.[2] These attacks on the lives of residents of our state were the result of federal, county, and city coordination in immigration enforcement efforts, a decentralized approach that deputized local police to enforce federal laws.

In a 2010 report, researchers at the University of North Carolina at Chapel Hill (UNC) discovered that, of all the states in the country, ours had the most county and municipal jurisdictions participate in the federal 287(g) ICE ACCESS program. The 287(g) program authorized local officers, in collaboration with the Department of Homeland Security (DHS), "to detect, detain, and deport" undocumented residents.[3] "This decentralization of responsibility over immigration enforcement—from Federal to State and Local governments—is radically transforming the immigration policy landscape," the authors of the UNC study observed.[4] They continued, "In addition to the 287(g) Program, the Department of Homeland Security is piloting a similar initiative in the state called Secure Communities and plans to implement this program nationwide over the next four years. As a result, North Carolina is an important laboratory for examining the implementation of local immigration governance."[5] A group of us didn't want our communities to become laboratories for anti-immigrant experiments. As people living on the front lines of an ever-expanding war on immigrants, we decided to look for points of resistance to disrupt their plans.[6]

Jacqueline Stevens, a political scientist who had been tracking ICE's expansion, published online a list of detention centers—unmarked field offices hidden in plain sight—including one in a section of suburban sprawl in Cary, between Durham and Raleigh. "ICE's low-lying brick building with a bright blue awning has darkened windows, no sign and no US flag. . . . The office complex has perhaps twenty other businesses, all of which do have signs," Stevens reported in the *Nation*.[7] "People in shackles and handcuffs are shuffled in from the rear."[8] That ICE would conceal these short-term detention centers from public scrutiny fit within their overall posture of secrecy. As an executive director for ICE, James Pendergraph informed staff from police and sheriff departments at a 2008 national law enforcement conference, "If you don't have enough evidence to charge someone criminally but you think he's illegal, we can make him disappear."[9]

To disappear people. To vanish neighbors from society. Pendergraph's offer for ICE to get rid of community members recalled to our minds stories from the 1970s and 1980s in South America, when the US military participated in state-sponsored kidnappings and torture to prop up right-wing regimes that were aligned with US interests. The Central Intelligence Agency took on the role of organizing these covert operations, named Operation Condor, with the US Army's School of the Americas in Ft. Benning, Georgia, as the hub for foreign military officers to learn methods of torture and tactics for repression. From this school, the leaders of military dictatorships in Argentina, Chile, Uruguay, Paraguay, Bolivia, and Brazil unleashed death squads, experts in the violent methods of disappearance, all under the auspices of the United States' anti-communist politics. In the wake of these terrors, communities within these countries organized protests and searches for *los desaparecidos*, hoping for reunion with disappeared loved ones while dreading the news of a discovery of one more mass grave. *We can make him disappear*—with those words, Pendergraph roused memories from a frightening era, a throwback to a US security apparatus feared throughout the Americas.

That year, in 2010, as Holy Week approached, we organized a foot-washing worship service for Maundy Thursday on the premises of the ICE field office in Cary—the site Jacqueline Stevens had identified in her reporting. The Thursday of Holy Week remembers Jesus's last meal with his disciples, when he washed the feet of his friends as a sign of his servanthood and love and told them to do the same for each other in his absence. Christians everywhere repeat that ritual in their churches as they prepare for Easter; we would host our service in ICE's parking lot and ask to wash the feet of the detained.

We parked our cars around a cul-de-sac in a nondescript business park. Our crowd of fifty people walked down a driveway to a two-story brick office with tinted windows. The building looked unoccupied, except for all the white vans with government license plates parked around the building. At the back, behind the office, we set up our basins and jugs of water in front of the intake gates where ICE vehicles would unload detainees to be processed. A member of our organizing committee, Patrick, walked up to the front entrance to ask permission for us to wash the feet of the detainees. They had locked the office, which we had anticipated, so he slipped our written request through the slim gap under the reinforced door. Meanwhile, behind the building, I passed around hymnals and slips of paper with our order of worship.

With the gathered body in a semicircle around the two water basins and chairs, we began our service with prayer. "Liberating God," we said in unison, "Let your will be done, let those who mourn be comforted and those in bondage be set free."[10] Then we read lines from Psalm 146 as a call and response: "Do not put your trust in princes, . . . in whom there is no help. . . . The Lord sets the prisoners free" (3, 7). I flipped the pages of my Bible to the Gospel of John, chapter 13, and read the foot-washing story. Before I invited people to come forward for me to wash their feet, I offered a short reflection on the meaning of the passage, given that our service was taking place outside an ICE field office. "Bodies matter for Jesus," I preached. "He shows his love for us by washing feet, by taking our bodies into his hands. And he commands us to go and do likewise, to love our neighbors with our actions, with our . . ." Then, suddenly, squad cars squealed around the building, officers from the Cary Police Department— their blaring sirens stopping me mid-sentence. We had prepared for this interruption. As organizers of the event, we were committed to going through with the worship service, even if that would mean our arrest. We knew the potential consequences for our organized petition to God and the political authorities for peace.

An officer walked through the crowd and stepped in front of me. "You must stop now and leave these premises immediately!" I stepped to the side of him, took a deep breath, and continued my sermon. "We are here to draw near to our neighbors confined in this building," I continued to speak to our assembled community, "to draw as close as possible to the people separated from us." The officer paced around me, yelling at the crowd, "All right, we're done here; you all have to leave now." Then he turned to me, "Are you in charge?" My voice trembled as I addressed the worship participants again. "We are here to proclaim the love of Christ, for God so loved the world, and that means everybody, even those whom our government takes from us." While I went on with my sermon, a member of our organizing committee distracted the officer with questions about the law. She drew the man into an argumentative discussion about the right to assembly and access to public space—a hushed sideshow at the edge of the crowd.

At the periphery of our gathering, other police officers brooded, agitated at our stubborn persistence, and awaited orders. With our forced dispersal imminent, I cut my sermon short and transitioned to the foot-washing part of the service, the culmination of our worship. "This chair here will remain empty as

a sign of an absence," I pointed to one of the two chairs behind
me. "An empty chair to remember all of the people who've been
torn from our families and neighborhoods and churches." I lifted
one of the pitchers of water. "In this holy act, we bear witness to
God's love for us and for those who've been taken from us, leaving us wounded, dismembered, with holes in our hands and side:
the pierced and severed body of Christ." With those words I took
my place, kneeling, at one of the chairs, with a gallon jug of water
and a stack of towels beside me. I held in my hands the feet of
each person in line, one after another, washing and drying them.
Next to me, the other chair remained empty—a holy absence.

"All of you must immediately disperse," an officer shouted from
a megaphone. "If you do not disperse, you will be subject to arrest."
The harsh sound interrupted the peacefulness of the moment.
I stood up from my bowed position at a person's feet, someone who
had waited in the foot-washing line for a while, and I let everyone
know that they should head back to their cars if they didn't want
to risk arrest and a potential misdemeanor. But, I added, I would
stay at the chairs until I finished washing the feet of anyone who
still wanted to participate. Some walked back up the driveway to
the cul-de-sac; most stayed for the conclusion of the service.

As I finished drying the feet of the last person, an officer
blasted orders from the megaphone again. "This is your last
warning," he announced. "You must disperse immediately. If
you do not, you will be arrested." Of the people who remained,
no one moved. I got up from my knees, faced our group, and
invited everyone to turn to the back of their bulletins for our
closing litany. "To the prisoners with whom Christ dwells, we
pledge allegiance," we proclaimed. "To the one who rules with
a towel rather than a gun and handcuffs, we pledge allegiance.
To the Way that leads to life for all people no matter where they

are born, we pledge allegiance."[11] Despite their bluster, the police left us alone; no one was arrested. I concluded the service with a benediction and asked several people to help me carry our chairs and basins and towels back to my car. Our exit was somber, dirge-like—our procession was a lament for the ongoing violence perpetrated by our government.[12]

For people committed to the noncoercive peace of Christ, worship prophesies a world transfigured with God's justice. There, in the ICE parking lot, we assembled to declare our solidarity with undocumented neighbors and to conjure a political imagination for a society without deportation. With our act of worship, we laid claim to a spot in the political terrain from which we could name the gap between the world we want and the one we have—a gap that is like a wound in our body politic, a social severing. Our liturgy was a plea for God to heal our communities from the harmful politics of zealous nationalism, from the nation-state's fervent belief in self-preservation at all costs, including a reliance on the violence of anti-immigrant policies. And we hoped that our citizen-neighbors would overhear our prayers, that they'd join us in the struggle for transformation and would lend their hands to the work of shifting our country away from an identity that depends on the banishment of the people our legal structure designates as "aliens."

To wash each other's feet, as Jesus taught us to do, is a confession of love for our neighbors. With our hands and feet, with water and towels, we profess our hope in the possibility of a world where we can live together in peace. We learn our Christian witness from the posture of foot washing: a politics of care, of gentleness, and a commitment to our neighbors—to surround each other with communities for life, regardless of the dictates of citizenship's hierarchies of belonging.

We returned to that site, year after year, during Obama's administration, to proclaim our belief in a way of life that doesn't require the violence of detention and deportation. Then Donald Trump was elected president.

Panic shot through our communities. Undocumented neighbors, already under threat, experienced a new level of alarm. Their homes and families were in peril; their lives in this country were in danger. Energy shifted from protests to community defense. Within months of Trump's election, outraged citizens who hadn't been involved in the immigrant justice movement quickly joined advocacy groups and solidarity coalitions. Existing organizations channeled their work toward partnerships with immigrant-led groups.

That's how I heard about Carolina Jews for Justice (CJJ), a grassroots network founded in 2013, centered on the Jewish commitment to *tikkun olam*—the repair of the world, and justice as the restoration of our wholeness, of our peaceable relations. In response to the Trump administration's attack on undocumented people, and with the Torah as their guide, CJJ called upon their membership across the state to join them in immigration advocacy work. "As North Carolinians and as Jews," they wrote, "we are committed to welcoming all who seek the same promise of safety and prosperity that first drew many of our own ancestors to this land. One of our core guiding principles at CJJ is *V'ahavta L'reacha Kamocha* (*love your neighbor as yourself*)."[13] They partnered with Mijente, a national Latinx and Chicanx justice organization, and Siembra NC, a state-wide collective of Latiné residents "with or without papers," to protest against the administration's abusive politics nationally and to engage in community defense work against ICE's incursions locally.[14]

In July 2018, CJJ mobilized Jews in North Carolina to join Mijente's mass demonstration in San Diego, California, to shut down a federal building that served as a regional hub for Operation Streamline, a judicial program established to rush migrants *en masse* through legal proceedings in order to fast-track their conviction and deportation.[15] In November 2019, CJJ partnered with Siembra NC to organize a protest in Graham against the sheriff's contract with ICE to imprison undocumented immigrants in the county detention center. "Many of those in our movement are Jewish people whose ancestors faced conditions disturbingly similar to what we are seeing today at the border and in detention centers around the country," the organizers wrote in their announcement. "We know from our own history what happens when a government targets, dehumanizes and strips an entire group of people of their civil and human rights."[16] The event was part of a national campaign called Never Again Action, a movement of Jews across the country who were disturbed by the Trump administration's all-out attack on immigrants. "As Jews, we carry both our ancestors' memories of persecution and the fierceness of their resistance," the Never Again collective stated. "We know fascism when we see it, and we know that no one is free until everyone is free."[17]

During these desperate times, in the midst of their advocacy and activism, CJJ stayed grounded in their religious tradition. In the summer of 2018, they hosted a Tisha B'Av service for the Jewish community in Durham and extended an invitation to those of us who had joined in their immigrant justice work. On the evening of the ninth day of the month of Av, according to the Jewish calendar, we gathered in front of the courthouse downtown. We all wore black. Many were also fasting, as is common for this day set aside to remember and mourn the destruction of the Temple in Jerusalem first in 586 BCE and again in 70 CE. This service would lament both the catastrophes of the past and the terrors of the present as we reeled from the havoc in our community.

We arrived in silence, each person finding a spot to sit on the blankets in the courthouse's plaza. "Our own history is filled with stories of displacement, of communities torn apart," the rabbi called out into the night. "We gather here to commemorate these historic tragedies and call for an end to the ongoing tragedy in this country, where families are torn apart and asylum seekers are denied refuge." With these words she began the service of prayer, centering us on passages from the scroll of Eicha, the book of Lamentations, with several verses read as a call and response.

> My eyes are spent with tears, my heart is in tumult.
> My being melts away over the ruin of my people.
> Far from me is any comforter who might revive
>   my spirit.
> My children are forlorn, for the foe has prevailed. (2:11)

The rabbi invited someone in the crowd to read an account from a Guatemalan woman, confined in Stewart Detention Center in Georgia. We responded with a verse from the first chapter of Lamentations, "Hear, all you peoples, and behold my agony: my girls and boys have gone into captivity" (1:18).

In her book *Opening Israel's Scriptures*, Ellen Davis describes the genre of Lamentations as "disaster poetry." "When a people has suffered the dehumanizing loss that war entails," she writes, "when precious bodies are broken and discarded like clay pots, then the most rehumanizing thing a writer can do is express love and longing for what is lost."[18] During the Tisha B'Av service, the Jewish community prayed through the verses of Lamentations as a collective act of mourning for the histories of violence and persecution, of genocide and expulsion, of deportation and exile—of disaster. Their supplications were love poems for broken bodies and stolen lives, a service to remember the dead and long for restoration. "Return us to You, O God," the poet of Eicha prays. "Renew our days like the dawn" (5:21).

There, in the courtyard, as nightfall shrouded us with darkness, the rabbi passed around a box of taper candles. Each of us turned to the people around us to light our wicks as the one flame became many. "Blessed are You, Adonai, our God, Ruler of the universe, Creator of the fire's light," she prayed over our candles, her face toward the dark sky. Soon we read out the names of the dead—people who had died in ICE's detention centers and migrants who had been killed by Border Patrol agents. The rabbi offered a prayer to mourn the loss of so many lives—the Kaddish for the dead, for these people we named as well as for the unnamed multitudes who had died in the US-Mexico borderlands.

A member of the CJJ community then read a prayer by Tamar Fox, "A Prayer for Undocumented Families Torn Apart," which she wrote for groups to use in the Jewish rituals of mourning and remembrance taking place across the country. "*Avinu malkeinu*, our parent, who shepherded us through the wilderness, sheltered us from evil," a reader prayed on our behalf, "we cry out to you now for families in the wilderness, children plucked from the arms of their loving parents, young people living behind bars."[19] By candlelight our group processed up the sidewalk into the heart of our downtown as we recited *kinot*, dirges for the dead. "Oy, meh haya lanu" (Oh, what has befallen us), our anguished song echoed through the streets.

To conclude the service we circled together. I glanced at
the people around me, each face aglow as our candles' flames
danced in the darkness. The words of a poem flashed through
my mind, the last stanza from Havah Eshel's "Tisha B'Av,"

> then circle circle
> and circle again
> till light meets light
> in a new ceremony
> of temple building love.[20]

That night the lamentation of the Jewish community reached out
to all who were suffering from our country's immigration policies—a ceremony of spiritual embrace, circles of light, the flick-
ers of love and solidarity. Hope felt like the warmth of neighbors
who cried out for *tikkun olam*, for the repair of our world. That
evening the diasporic assembly included in their prayers people
whose lives had been crushed at the hands of ICE agents, Border
Patrol officers, and detention center guards. Along with elegies
for Jerusalem, the holy ritual remembered the thousands of children in cages across the country, the reports of sexual abuse in
detention centers, and the asylum seekers sent back to brave
another attempt at crossing the border, to try again at survival
in this ruthless world.

After the service I asked Dove Kent, a member of CJJ who
helped organize the service, about her own sense of the need to
remember current oppressions as part of the observance of Tisha
B'Av. "The stories that we pass down in Jewish tradition, of our
persecution and expulsion, teach our hearts to remain open," she
told me. "When we see immigrants hunted down and expelled

from our country, they are not separate from us because our stories belong to each other."

The words from the Tisha B'Av service, from Lamentations, echoed through our neighborhoods as a call for protection from the harms of deportation. "Even now our eyes pine away in vain for deliverance," we prayed. "Still we wait for a nation that will not help" (Lam. 4:17).

These were devastating years, one catastrophe after another. There were and still are ruins everywhere. Yet, despite the assaults, here in our country immigrant communities have persevered.

- 5 -

COMMUNITY DEFENSE

I walked toward the five cars clustered together at the far end of the Hardee's parking lot. As I approached one, the driver and passenger rolled up their windows. I stood at the driver's side, smiled and waved, and asked a question. The person acknowledged my presence by quickly reaching his hand to shut the steel-plated laptop bolted into a console between the driver's and passenger's seats. Then he pulled his car away, heading for the exit. Each of the other drivers followed his lead. They scattered, darting their vehicles into the bustle of morning traffic.

Our community defense network had been tracking ICE operations across the state for the past several weeks as federal agents converged upon several metropolitan counties in North Carolina, including the Triangle: the tri-city region of Raleigh, Durham, and Chapel Hill. "This is a direct conclusion of dangerous policies of not cooperating with ICE," Sean Gallagher, the ICE field office director, said at a press conference in February 2019.[1] As the overseer of operations for the Carolinas, he had already promised to retaliate with raids in our communities if our newly elected sheriffs didn't cooperate with his ICE office—in December 2018 he had threatened "additional collateral arrests." "ICE will now have no choice but to conduct more at-large arrests in local neighborhoods and at worksites," an official from Gallagher's office warned.[2]

Gary McFadden, the newly elected sheriff of Mecklenburg County, would not back down from his campaign promise to the residents of Charlotte, the largest city in our state. Upon his election he joined immigration justice advocates at a Latino bakery where the owner, a Colombian immigrant, had made a sheet cake with a crossed-out "287(g)" written with frosting in the middle.[3] Sheriff McFadden signed the termination documents for his county's existing cooperation agreement, then picked up a kitchen knife and cut across the cake, slicing through the 287(g) at the center. A new sheriff was in town, one who refused to partner with ICE.[4]

Within two months, in an act of retribution, Gallagher's agents unleashed their fury—not only in Charlotte but also in other noncooperative counties, including ours, Durham County. After a week of raids throughout the state, federal officers arrested over two hundred people and transported them to detention facilities to begin the judicial machinations that would conclude in deportation. This would be "the new normal," as the Assistant Field Office Director Robert Alfieri described the weeklong blitz.[5]

In the middle of their rampage, an undocumented neighbor let me know that several workers on her husband's construction crew had seen plainclothes officers meet for breakfast at Hardee's, then head out as a fleet of four or five vehicles into the surrounding communities. I posted the tip to our community defense texting group. Within the hour we had developed a plan for our members to station themselves there—one-hour shifts from dawn to mid-morning—as ICE watchers. That was how I managed to arrive at the Hardee's parking lot in time to talk with the agents—to *try* to talk with them. Before this encounter, our rapid response teams had always shown up late to their operations in our community—there for the aftermath of an arrest, in the wake of an abduction. This time, however, we managed to orchestrate a confrontation.

Information sharing with immigration justice coalitions in other parts of the United States helped us realize that ICE agents fear scrutiny and that confrontations with people who would record their activity with cell phones were enough to disband them. They scatter in the light, afraid of their exposure to the public, because ICE agents know that they operate at the limits of questionable laws.

The racial diversity of our urban life in Durham makes us who we are, as a people, as a community. We cherish our identity enough to organize against the kind of policing that threatens the well-being of our common life. Through her research on immigration and incarceration, Kelly Lytle Hernández has investigated the nexus of racism and policing. She has attended to the fundamental role border enforcement has played in our carceral society. "Historically speaking," Hernández argues, "immigration control is one of the least constitutional and most racist realms of governance in U.S. law and life."[6] ICE agents, as the latest version of *la migra*, guard the racialized borders of this country. Immigration police are on the front lines of a culture war about the ethnic composition of our neighborhoods and schools. Immigration policies and policing are about cultural formation, the making of a peoplehood—a racial politics that reaches into the intimacies of our friendships and the makeup of our families, the segregated geographies that regulate who might fall in love with whom, the landscapes of our kinship. *La migra* patrol the boundaries of citizenship, of belonging.

Over the past decade, our grassroots activism has shifted the political culture of our city—as reflected both in municipal policies and in the discourse of our elected officials. I remember our immigrant justice coalitions packing the room for a city council session in 2010, for the public discussion about a proposal to endorse a particular Mexican ID, the Matricula Consular, as an acceptable identification card in our municipality. Two councillors voted against the proposal. Each took the opportunity to explain their opposition in their own words. One of them, an esteemed civil rights icon, firmly declared that the ID was an inappropriate attempt for people who've been identified as "less than citizens" to "validate their existence as part of the Durham community."[7] Over the past nine years that sentiment, expressed by an elected representative, has receded from public forums. Instead, our elected officials now name all residents, regardless of documentation status, as within the purview of their constituencies—a political responsibility not only to citizens who vote but to all the people who make Durham life possible. Public servants no longer point to a person's federal documentation as authorization for belonging here. Local representatives don't appeal to legal papers as part of their calculations to determine a person's validation as a member of our city, as beloved in our community.

This time—in 2019, during the raids—when the federal status of undocumented people was thrust into the consciousness of local politics again, our mayor released a statement on behalf of the city council decrying ICE's incursions. "The ICE raids have struck terror in the hearts of many of our valued community members. They have broken apart families, separating parents from their children," Mayor Steve Schewel declared, along with six other mayors across the state who co-signed his statement. "We cannot stop ICE from operating in our cities, but we can and must speak out against these raids which destabilize neighborhoods [and] traumatize children."[8] Our county commissioners followed this proclamation of solidarity with their own statement: "The Durham County Board of Commissioners strongly condemns the recent ICE actions in the Durham community which have directly impacted at least 6 families in Durham," the chair read on behalf of the board. "These actions by ICE do not serve to make the Durham community safer. In fact, they serve to terrorize the immigrant and Latinx community in Durham to the point that it makes our community less safe."[9]

Safety from terror and trauma—this need for the well-being of our people prompted us to form our community defense coalition, an informal network of documented and undocumented residents prepared to protect neighbors who had been targeted for deportation. In response to President Trump's malice against immigrants, our rapid-response collective emerged—with safe houses for people who couldn't go home due to the surveillance of immigration police, and trained volunteers ready for dispatch whenever someone called our hotline to report an ICE sighting. We weren't alone in our work. People across the country were joining a movement of "sanctuary cities."

Sanctuary as a tactic for political resistance comes from the Christian story, from a long tradition of churches that would harbor people in need of protection from punishment. In 441 CE, for example, Bishop Hilary of Arles convened a provincial synod in France, the Council of Orange, which authorized the protection of fugitives who sought asylum in church buildings. "If any one has taken refuge in a church he shall not be given up, but shall be sheltered from respect to the sacred place," the council declared in their fifth canon.[10] In his *Sanctuary and Crime in the Middle Ages, 400–1500*, legal historian Karl Shoemaker tells the story of the formation of this tradition of ecclesial sanctuary, of congregations offering their properties as places of refuge from the violence of the law.[11] In the United States, late in the twentieth century, church members read this medieval tradition alongside the Black abolitionist movement as inspiration for harboring Central Americans who had to flee for survival from US-sponsored warfare in their home countries—*Sanctuary: The New Underground Railroad*, as Renny Golden and Michael McConnell titled their 1986 account of that era of activism. "The sanctuary movement has arisen in a nation that trains and arms the killers of innocent persons," they wrote, "and then deems it criminal to shelter the victims of that slaughter."[12] Our sanctuary efforts, whether in places of worship or in secular organizing, extended this tradition into our own resistance against the violent politics of detention and deportation.

In the Hardee's parking lot, as the ICE agents fled in their cars and vans, I rushed after them—down a main road and into a neighborhood. The driver pulled around the back of an old Lutheran church, behind the main building. I waited in my car across the street until I noticed several of the other vehicles I had seen at Hardee's join him. I drove up beside them, parked, and walked to a blue jeep—to the driver's side. The man's arm hung out the window. "Hello," I greeted him, "my name is Isaac Villegas. I live down the street." He pulled his arm inside and glanced at the man in the passenger's seat. "Are you an ICE agent?" I asked. He looked at me, blankly. Between them there was a laptop apparatus, similar to the one I had seen in the car at Hardee's. "Are you a federal employee?" I persisted. He shifted away from the window and tilted his head to his colleague; they shared a slight nod, a knowingness, making an unspoken decision. The driver then turned the key in the ignition and sped off. The other vehicles followed, screeching out of the Lutheran parking lot. I got into my car and followed one of them for as long as I could keep up. He must have seen me in his rearview mirror because he accelerated, suddenly, to race through an intersection as the light turned red. I decided a chase wasn't wise or appropriate—not worth the risk of safety for everyone around, including ourselves. I had read accounts of ICE's reckless behavior on the roads. In the previous year, for example, in California's Central Valley, ICE officers lied about a deadly car accident they had instigated during a pursuit at dangerous speeds. The attempted apprehension turned out to be a case of mistaken identities.[13]

ICE agents prowl through our communities on clandestine operations, trying to evade public awareness and accountability, in pursuit of undocumented people. This federal obsession with the documentation of certain residents extends the long US tradition of racialized surveillance—strategies to control Black populations redeployed against migrants. "For the black subject," Simone Browne explains in *Dark Matters: On the Surveillance of Blackness*, "the potentiality of being under watch was a cumulative effect of the large-scale surveillance apparatus in colonial New York City and beyond, stemming from transatlantic slavery."[14] Browne describes the emergence of identity documents in the early republic as how the authorities established who, within the Black population, was allowed the freedom of movement.[15] The Treaty of Paris in 1783 stipulated the freedom of Black Loyalists in the American colonies; the agreement ensured that they would not be appropriated as slaves by the revolutionary colonists. To ensure their freedom from capture, two British generals—first General Samuel Birch, then General Thomas Musgrave—issued certificates of safe passage in New York for Black residents of the colonies who were, or had become (by fleeing plantations during the War of Independence), subjects of the crown and therefore guaranteed for themselves a legal status of being unenslavable. These British documents were first called "Birch Certificates," then "Certificates of Freedom," and later were compiled into a ledger that became known as *The Book of Negroes*. These were early forms of international passports, and they provided Black people in the colonies the right of movement: to relocate north to Nova Scotia or to embark across the Atlantic to England. "The *Book of Negroes* is an early imprint of how the body comes to be understood as a means of identification and tracking by the state," Browne argues.[16]

This colonial desire to surveil and possess reached beyond Black communities. Indigenous life was also subject to the control of the European colonists. Browne describes the "Lantern Laws," as they came to be known, in New York City. In 1713 the city council passed the first piece of legislation, then revised the language in 1731, titled the "Law for Regulating Negro & Indian Slaves in the Night Time." The legal code stipulated the geographic areas accessible to "Negro, Mulatto or Native" populations of the region—where they were forbidden and where they could traverse during certain hours as long as the person carried a candle-lantern to identify themselves. The lantern requirement served as a kind of documentation status, a tracking system for policing non-European peoples, enslavable lives. "Lantern laws made the lit candle a supervisory device," Browne writes, "and part of the legal framework that marked black, mixed-race, and indigenous people as security risks."[17]

These motley groups posed a security threat to the colonial project in the so-called New World because, from the birth of the nation, the political architects of the United States structured the country as an ethno-state: that is, according to an ethnic nationalism whose boundaries required constant policing. "The origins of these concepts," argues legal historian Mae M. Ngai, "lay in the Nationality Act of 1790, which granted the right to naturalized citizenship to 'free white persons' of good moral character."[18] In her book *Impossible Subjects: Illegal Aliens and the Making of Modern America*, Ngai tracks the racial vision at work in the formation and development of a US political identity that has produced the category of "illegal alien" as concomitant to the promise of national belonging. Within the purview of US jurisprudence and statecraft, the non-European immigrant has been a consistent source of unease—the foreign resident prods the anxieties at the heart of nationalism. According to Ngai, the Chinese Exclusion Act of 1882 proved decisive in the racial construction of US citizenship: "Believing immigration to be a potential form of 'foreign aggression and encroachment,' the Court gave Congress absolute control over it as part of its authority over foreign relations."[19] Ngai summarizes the legal ramifications of the US Supreme Court's decisions in support of Chinese exclusion: "It ruled that aliens enter and remain in the United States only with 'the license, permission, and sufferance of Congress.'"[20] Foreignness was associated with aggression and perceived as a threat to preserving an ethno-European core to the US national identity.

The Immigration Act of 1924 (the Johnson-Reed Act) consolidated this racial commitment into a law that still sets the terms of our conversations about the nature of belonging in US society. "During the 1920s," Ngai writes, "the legal traditions that had justified racial discrimination against African Americans were extended to other ethno-racial groups in immigration law through the use of euphemism ('aliens ineligible to citizenship') and the invention of new categories of identity ('national origin')."[21] With this legislation, US law expanded the scope of its legacy of anti-Blackness to include non-European immigrants. While Browne traces the invention of the modern passport to the surveillance of Black and Native peoples in the North American colonies, Ngai notes that international passports developed on a global scale in the context of warfare—first as emergency war measures during World War I in order to process and track European refugees, and then in the aftermath of that war as nation-states began to work out the scope of their sovereignty over land and people.[22]

With the inclusion of this novel category of "national origin," the 1924 law structured an immigration system according to nativism, an ideology that centered—and continues to center—people of European ancestry as the self-appointed heirs of our national polity. The legislation set up quotas according to a person's birthplace; these determined whether migrants would be allowed to seek citizenship in the United States. The quotas prioritized populations from Europe to the exclusion of Latin American and Asian peoples, which allowed nativists "to devise a plan that would discriminate without appearing to do so."[23] A racism without racists, to borrow Eduardo Bonilla-Silva's phrase.[24]

Ngai outlines the political effects of the nativist impulse enshrined in this early twentieth-century law: "The Immigration Act of 1924 constructed a vision of the American nation that embodied certain hierarchies of race and nationality," which "served contemporary prejudices among white Protestant Americans"—an essential sanction for "their desire to maintain social and political dominance."[25] She explains, in summary, "The law constructed a white American race, in which persons of European descent shared a common whiteness distinct from those deemed to be not white."[26] In a series of decisions regarding property rights, the Supreme Court mapped out the legal terrain for Congress to build the Immigration Act. In California and Washington, notes Ngai, white panic at the influx of foreigners resulted in "Alien Land Laws" that prohibited primarily Japanese immigrants, as well as other people of Asian descent, from ownership of land. As the Court claimed in the *Terrance v. Thompson* decision in 1923, "One who is not a citizen and cannot become one lacks an interest in, and the power to effectively work for the welfare of the state, and so lacking, the state may rightfully deny him the right to own or lease land estate within its boundaries. If one incapable of citizenship may lease or own real estate, it is within the realm of possibility that every foot of land within the state may pass to the ownership of non-citizens."[27] This legal framework was revised with the Immigration and Nationality Act of 1952 (the McCarran-Walter Act) and finally replaced in the Immigration and Nationality Act of 1965 (the Hart-Celler Act), which finally abolished the criterion of national origins as the basis for immigration quotas.[28]

While the most overtly racist pieces of the 1924 legislation were removed from the updated Immigration and Nationality Act of 1965, the direction of the legal framework remained the same: to empower immigration police as they arrest, detain, and deport, all as part of maintaining the rights and privileges of citizenship for some residents instead of others. The effect of those laws has not been undone. The permission to discriminate has already been unleashed, a political disposition that continues to inhabit our society.[29]

This racialized world first imposed itself upon me when, as a child, Border Patrol agents detained my family at a checkpoint on Interstate 8 in a desolate stretch of the Californian landscape. They took my Colombian father away for questioning while my Costa Rican mother looked after my sister and me. We waited for what felt like hours in the parking lot of an inspection zone, watching the police dogs sniff our van, our seats, and our backpacks. *La migra* was white; we were brown. Accents rendered us suspect. Skin color made us eligible for interrogation. There, on the side of the highway, the dogs and their handlers taught me my racial difference.

To maintain these distinctions, immigration officers now patrol the interior of the country, not only the edges. The border is no longer at the border. In *The End of the Myth: From the Frontier to the Border Wall in the Mind of America*, historian Greg Grandin puts on display the anxieties of a colonial imagination still at work in our society, with first the frontier and now the border wall as announcements of "the panic of power" internal to US statecraft, a governance "constantly in danger of being undone."[30] In recent history, President Trump embodied this frail colonial egoism as he lashed out at migrants—a tantrum politics, trembling with violence—which resonated with large swaths of voters. Trump, however, is not an outlier to the vision for this country that Grandin describes as "Jacksonian," a politics of liberty conceived as a (white) citizen's right to "freedom from restraint."[31] This disposition has been the bedrock of US political freedom from the beginning as "settlers moved across the frontier, continuing to win a greater freedom by putting down people of color," Grandin writes, "and then continuing to define their liberty in opposition to the people of color they put down."[32] To secure this freedom for the citizen involved the containment of migrants. To defend the citizen's rights entailed a politics that positioned the immigrant as suspicious, as a potential enemy to American freedom.

I remember, as a teenager, President Bill Clinton's articulation of this vision in his State of the Union address on January 24, 1995:

> All Americans, not only in the states most heavily affected but in every place in this country, are rightly disturbed by the large numbers of illegal aliens entering our country. The jobs they hold might otherwise be held by citizens or legal immigrants. The public services they use impose burdens on our taxpayers. That's why our administration has moved aggressively to secure our borders more by hiring a record number of new border guards, by deporting twice as many criminal aliens as ever before, by cracking down on illegal hiring, by barring welfare benefits to illegal aliens.[33]

His fearmongering about people at the border prefigured the rhetoric of President Trump. In this speech, President Clinton promised a Trumpian America. Or, perhaps we should say Trump is Clintonian—Trump was faithful to Clinton's vision for a society that obstructs the belonging of immigrants. There are differences, of course. Clinton's discourse remained in the economic register, whereas Trump has depicted immigrants as a violent horde, a menace to the social fabric of the United States, and an existential danger to the greatness of American freedom.

For political leaders—in their rhetoric and policies—to render migrants as a threat has empowered the vitriol of anti-immigrant citizens. Grandin recounts the efforts of white supremacists and militias to organize extrajudicial patrols in defense of their ethno-nationalist dreams—from the Ku Klux Klan terrorizing Latiné communities and migrant camps ("beaner raids," they called the incursions), including a young David Duke setting up the Klan's "border watch" near San Ysidro, California, to the Minutemen movement of civilians who conduct extrajudicial border enforcement operations.[34] Grandin documents how these groups have now stationed themselves throughout the continental United States. "'The border is no longer in the desert,' the founder of Kansas City's 'Heart of America' Minuteman Civil Defense Corps chapter said. 'It is all over America.' By the end of 2006," Grandin continues, "according to one count, one hundred forty Minuteman branches had been established in thirty-four states."[35] Armed militias have commissioned themselves as auxiliary units of US immigration police—a united front, without coordination, against migrants.

On August 3, 2019, a Dallas resident posted in a white supremacist chat group online a screed against Latiné people in the United States and against interracial marriage. "This attack," he announced, "is a response to the Hispanic invasion of Texas. They are the instigators, not me. I am simply defending my country from cultural and ethnic replacement brought on by the invasion."[36] Twenty minutes later, he entered a Walmart in El Paso—he must have posted his online manifesto from the parking lot—and hunted down brown people, killing twenty-two individuals and injuring another twenty-six.[37] The next week President Trump condemned the massacre, a requisite statement for the presidential office.[38] Then, later that month—with victims still in the hospital, with family and friends still in mourning—he revived his call for the abolition of birthright citizenship, an impossible demand since the proposal would involve changing the Fourteenth Amendment to the US Constitution, which guarantees the automatic citizenship of anyone born in the United States (for example, me), regardless of the parents' legal status. The feasibility of his proposal wasn't the point. Instead, this was one of Trump's signals to his electorate, another opportunity for him to stoke the rage of his anti-immigrant supporters.[39]

When the president loosed ICE agents in North Carolina—to instill fear among immigrants and rally his base with promises of a nativist future—solidarity networks organized vigilance in our communities. Mutual care was our natural reaction to Trump's attempt to sever us, to tear apart our peoplehood. Community defense is the reflexive politics of self-protection—vigilance as a collective posture of antiviolence, to preserve a society from those who seek destruction. We became sentinels, ready to alert people about ICE's activities.

The biblical prophet Ezekiel called for posting a sentinel for the community, one who "blows the trumpet and warns the people" (Ezek. 33:1-6). Gardner C. Taylor, in his Beecher Lectures, included this role of the watcher as part of the task of the preacher—the prophetic as pastoral.[40] In other words, "The shepherd is someone who keeps watch," as Michel Foucault summarizes the biblical imagery regarding the appointment of some to look out for the safety, the salvation—*salut*, in Foucault's French, includes both meanings, "safety" and "salvation," as does biblical Hebrew—of the whole community.[41] The pastor "will keep watch over the flock and avoid the misfortune that may threaten the least of its members."[42] Our community defense work has felt like a kind of pastoral care, where we become sentinels for each other, watchers appointed by neighbors to stay alert and sound the alarm when our people are in danger.

In the aftermath of the ICE raids, Councilwoman Javiera Caballero, the first Latina elected to Durham's city council, convened a group (activists, organizers, attorneys, a pastor—all of us immigrants or the children of immigrants) to strategize how to help pick up the pieces of the shattered lives of our neighbors. Community defense transitioned into mutual aid as we designed a solidarity fund for undocumented residents—a fund for housing assistance and detention bonds, for utility bills and groceries, for whatever our people needed to survive after ICE agents had taken a family member. In 2021, as needs shifted, we expanded the fund to support undocumented immigrants who had suffered financial loss due to the COVID-19 pandemic. In 2022, due to the interconnectedness of our communities, the fund was extended across our state. By the end of 2023, we had redistributed more than $1 million over four years. Our solidarity work, which emerged in response to Trump's anti-immigrant policies, generated structures of mutual care across the local political landscape—a societal ecosystem that included grassroots coalitions, nonprofit organizations, and municipal government programs.

The community we want is already here, among us, in our neighborhoods and workplaces. As immigrants and nonimmigrants who've stitched our lives into the fabric of society, we've become the peoplehood we want—perhaps only here and there, our fragile lives torn apart whenever politicians hungry for power repurpose old rallying cries in order to activate the worst of our nostalgic imaginations for a republic without foreigners. Community defense is what we do, in nonviolent resistance against forces that threaten our collective well-being, as we hope for a world without our neighbors having to live in constant fear of deportation.

We take turns, depending on the season, as each other's shepherds.

· 6 ·

SANCTUARY

For half of Trump's tenure as president, from April 2018 to February 2020, I slept at church one night a week. Some months more often, some months less. We set up a cot with a lumpy mattress in the corner of a large room, previously a prayer chapel. A crick in my lower back became a normal part of life from those fitful nights of "sleep." I was there, week after week, month after month, year after year, as one among a multitude of volunteers who provided overnight accompaniment for Rosa del Carmen Ortez-Cruz. Rosa lived on church property. Her room was between the old chapel and the current sanctuary. We had remodeled an office into her bedroom and converted a utility room into her bathroom.

Rosa lived at church for almost two years because, as soon as Trump took office, his administration included her among the thousands targeted for deportation. She moved into our church soon after ICE issued an official threat to arrest and remove her from the United States, to take her away from her children here in North Carolina and send her to Honduras, where she had fled the violence of an abuser fifteen years earlier. She found us because our congregation had declared ourselves available for protective, ecclesial sanctuary. We joined a coalition of churches that promised to protect undocumented residents of our community from federal deportation. In November 2016, as soon as US citizens elected Trump as the next president, I was on the road, meeting with pastors and talking to church groups throughout the state, enlisting their support and participation in communal acts of civil disobedience. By the time Trump was inaugurated, churches across North Carolina were at the ready to harbor and provide support for people in our communities on the run from his attacks on the undocumented among us. In 2018, during our most active months, we had six people at one time in public ecclesial sanctuary in our state—the most of any state.

In May 2017, Juana Tobar Ortega began her residence in St. Barnabas Episcopal Church in Greensboro. The next month, in Durham, José Chicas moved into a room at the School for Conversion, a religious nonprofit on the campus of St. John's Missionary Baptist Church. That October in Raleigh, Umstead Park United Church of Christ welcomed Eliseo Jimenez to live in their house of worship. In December, Samuel Oliver-Bruno entered CityWell United Methodist Church in Durham. In 2018, as the new year began, two more people declared sanctuary. Oscar Canales moved into Congregational United Church of Christ (Greensboro) in January, and Rosa del Carmen Ortez-Cruz found her way to our congregation in April.

Six people, all of whom had lived in North Carolina for years—some for decades, like José Chicas, who had fled the United States–sponsored civil war in El Salvador in the 1980s. All of them had been working on their legal cases for residency, until the election of Donald Trump cut the legs out from under them with a pair of executive orders—some of the first of his administration, as part of keeping his campaign promises. He directed DHS to arrest and deport anyone who did not have federal authorization to reside in this country. His orders on January 24, 2017—"Border Security and Immigration Enforcement Improvements" and "Enhancing Public Safety in the Interior of the United States"—granted immigration officers broad powers to deport unauthorized immigrants across the country. While President Obama had prioritized undocumented residents who had been convicted of serious crimes, President Trump provided comprehensive justifications for federal agents to flag people for deportation. His "enforcement priorities" included just about everyone without papers:

> In executing faithfully the immigration laws of the United States, the Secretary of Homeland Security (Secretary) shall prioritize for removal those aliens . . . who: (a) Have been convicted of any criminal offense; (b) Have been charged with any criminal offense, where such charge has not been resolved; (c) Have committed acts that constitute a chargeable criminal offense; (d) Have engaged in fraud or willful misrepresentation in connection with any official matter or application before a governmental agency; (e) Have abused any program related to receipt of public benefits; (f) Are subject to a final order of removal, but who have not complied with their legal obligation to depart the United States; or (g) In the judgment of an immigration officer, otherwise pose a risk to public safety or national security.[1]

The federal government's list of people to detain and deport started with an Obama-era priority but quickly widened under

Trump's administration to include just about anyone without official documentation. The criteria for a lawful arrest had now become whether an officer considered an undocumented person suspicious. No longer did someone have to be convicted or even charged with a crime. Instead, immigration agents were empowered to use their own judgment to determine whether someone was "a risk to public safety or national security." Even if local enforcement agencies did not charge someone with an offense, federal agents were authorized to detain undocumented people whom they considered to have "committed acts that constitute a chargeable criminal offense." Such wide parameters rendered everyone without documentation vulnerable to deportation proceedings.

Rosa's attorneys had been defending her against deportation for several years. Her case had to do with the protections offered in the United Nations' Convention Against Torture (CAT), an international treaty that forbids a country from deporting a person to a place from where they had originally escaped because of violence. In December 2000, while Rosa lived in Honduras where she was born, Rosa's partner stabbed her with a knife multiple times in her abdomen in an attempt to kill her. After emergency surgery and long weeks of recovery under the protection of the hospital, and as soon as she was healthy enough for the arduous journey, she fled north with her child to get as far away from her partner as possible. She went first to Mexico, then to the United States, where she settled in North Carolina, making a new life for herself. In 2013 DHS issued her a notice of removal, the first step in the government's process of deportation. That's when her attorney filed for protection under CAT, since her former partner in Honduras had sent her a message to let her know that he would kill her if he ever saw her again. Rosa's order of removal was put on hold while the courts deliberated her appeal. At the time, during Obama's administration, DHS did not consider it appropriate to interrupt the proceedings of the courts; ICE would pause their deportation operations to avoid interfering with a person's case. Rosa was safe with her family in North Carolina for as long as her case had merit. All of that changed when Trump was elected.

Rosa contacted me about the possibility of sanctuary in early 2018. Her attorney was suddenly faced with the new reality of ICE snatching away her clients, deporting them and thus cutting off their legal standing in the courts even though their cases were still in judicial proceedings. Her attorney was in the process of filing another appeal, but ICE officials had reissued their demand that Rosa leave the country despite the merits of her ongoing litigation. For Rosa to have a legal chance at freedom in the United States, for her to live without the daily threat of her ex-partner's violence, she would have to confine herself in a church, to live as a medieval anchoress in a modern world. At the recommendation of her attorney, Rosa called upon the solidarity of our congregation to protect her from deportation while her attorney persisted on her behalf in the courts.

Our church had been preparing for this moment. We were awaiting Rosa's call. We had organized our communal life as a prayer, an invitation, an offer of protective hospitality for undocumented people who were looking for safety—a secure place, a shelter. A year before her phone call, our congregation decided to offer public sanctuary as part of our community defense efforts against Trump's reinvigoration of ICE's incursions into cities and towns throughout the United States. Since we rent our location for worship from a Presbyterian church, we requested their permission to let us convert office space on their property into accommodations for a long-term resident, and we invited them to partner with us in the offer of sanctuary to an undocumented person. After several months of discernment, which involved wrestling with questions about insurance and finances and volunteer capacity, our two churches agreed to a covenant for our partnership as a way to articulate, as clearly as possible, our commitment to the people we would welcome together.

Then we began a construction overhaul. Church members reconfigured an office into a small apartment. We expanded the break room's kitchen to include the stuff needed for real cooking. A contractor from our congregation volunteered his time and skill to remodel a large utility closet into a full bathroom with a shower. We redesigned a prayer chapel across the hall from the new apartment into the volunteers' quarters, outfitted with the bed I already mentioned—my lower back still winces when I think about that mattress.

The night Rosa arrived, church member Xaris Martínez and I welcomed her. After we helped carry all her belongings from her friend's car to her room, we gathered in the common area for Xaris to offer a prayer. "Que la fuerza de Dios te mantenga firme," Xaris prayed, calling upon God's strength and protection as we rested our hands on Rosa's shoulders. "Que la Palabra de Dios te proteja a ti y a tu familia." I handed her a letter from Juana Tobar Ortega, who had already been living in sanctuary for a year at Saint Barnabas Episcopal in Greensboro, an hour's drive away. Later, a few days after Rosa's arrival, she had me read part of Juana's letter at our press conference, when we announced that she had decided to live in our protective care.

"Querida Rosa, no estamos solas"—with reporters and community members crowded into our worship sanctuary, and with Rosa beside me on the stage, I spoke Juana's words into the mic at the pulpit. "Dios apuesto ángeles a nuestro alrededor para ayudarnos a luchar" (God has surrounded us with angels). "Hemos luchado mucho para llegar aquí, para darles a nuestros hijos un futuro mejor" (We've endured so much in order to provide a better future for our children). "Así que luchemos por la libertad en este país que también es el nuestro" (So let's struggle for freedom in this country, which is also our county).

Juana knew the struggle ahead for Rosa. To sequester oneself on church property for months—for what would turn out to be nearly two years—takes physical and psychological fortitude. To wake up every morning and decide to stay one more day, in order to remain in this country, with the hope of a future with their children. Congregations had been considered safe from ICE's operations ever since the Obama presidency, when then ICE Director John Morton instructed agents not to trespass onto the grounds of worshiping communities as well as other "sensitive locations," in the language of Director Morton's memorandum.[2] That provided us with some reassurance that our church would be a refuge for Rosa, as long as ICE under Trump's administration would continue to follow the guidance of the Morton memo.

However, if agents did show up, we would be there to prevent them from taking her; we organized twenty-four-hour accompaniment. We would risk our own arrest to defend her. A church member, Lars Åkerson, designed a texting system that would alert subscribers to show up in a flash if we sent a call for help. All of us were ready to assemble ourselves as a shield of protection, to intercede on her behalf, and to stand in solidarity with her by blocking the entrance into the church building.

Rosa depended on us for the basics of life, for everyday necessities. Community members signed up for weekly errands and grocery runs. We designed a training program for those who wanted to join the accompaniment team—volunteers whom we would schedule for around-the-clock presence, including overnight shifts, to remain vigilant. In our training we made clear that accompaniment meant a responsibility to civil disobedience—to shield our resident from abduction. To offer sanctuary, I told our volunteers, involves a risk of prosecution. An overly eager federal prosecutor might feel empowered enough by the president's anti-immigrant agenda to charge some among us with harboring an unauthorized migrant. To drop off a casserole, I explained, might be taken as providing material support to an "illegal alien," which could be a prosecutable offense.[3] As Jesus says, we must count the personal costs of our discipleship before we engage in acts of faithfulness to God (Luke 14:28). For there may come a time when, like Peter and the apostles in Acts, we'll have to appear before the authorities and offer their same defense: "We must obey God rather than any human authority" (Acts 5:29). And Jesus was clear about the nature of our discipleship: to feed the hungry, to offer drink to the thirsty, to welcome the stranger, to clothe the needy, and to minister to the sick (Matt. 25:31–46). In other words, Christians are people who harbor and provide material comfort to anyone in need, including people our government categorizes as "illegal." With Rosa in our care, we understood our embodied witness of ecclesial sanctuary as a collective act of discipleship in opposition to the federal administration's anti-immigrant policies. Eleven congregations joined us in our coalition to support Rosa. In all, 160 volunteers regularly brought meals, helped with shopping, and provided accompaniment at the church, her home.

One afternoon, after a year at our church, Rosa called to let me know about a strange piece of mail she received from ICE.

The letter stated that she owed $314,007 in fines to the government: $799 for each day she had been in the United States without documentation. When I answered my phone, I was at our denominational convention walking with my friend Joel Miller, pastor of Columbus Mennonite Church (Ohio), where Edith Espinal was living in sanctuary. Before I called Rosa's attorney, I told him the shocking news. He phoned Edith and discovered that she had just received the same letter, although her fine was $497,777. In the next several hours, as we checked in with our network across the country, we discovered that ICE had sent notices of fines to nine of the forty-four people in public church sanctuary.[4] In the midst of our bewilderment, someone from the *New York Times* called me about the story. I asked if she knew why, out of nowhere, ICE had fined these particular people in sanctuary. The reporter said that she had spoken earlier with an official who seemed to shrug off the fines as standard practice.

A couple days later, in the published *New York Times* article, I read ICE Assistant Director of Public Affairs Carol Danko's statement: "ICE is committed to using various enforcement methods . . . to enforce U.S. immigration law."[5] According to Rosa's attorneys, DHS had used an ignored provision in the Immigration and Nationality Act of 1965—a forgotten stipulation that seasoned immigration attorneys had never seen used during their long careers. The government withdrew the fines for each of the nine people several months later, after our attorneys sent letters of protest indicating that they were prepared to sue the government. ICE never offered an explanation as to why they chose to pick out these nine people, not the dozens of others. Our best guess was that they targeted some of the more vocal people in sanctuary, perhaps as an intimidation tactic.[6]

Our ministry of sanctuary clashed with the Trump administration's agenda, but we knew that we were working with the grain of Christian tradition. Through the ages, churches have opened their doors to protect people. Places of worship became sanctuaries to preserve life. Augustine, the bishop of Hippo, recounts how church buildings served as havens as people tried to escape the onslaught of Alaric, the Visigoth king, when he invaded Rome in 410 CE. "The reliquaries of the martyrs and the churches of the apostles bear witness," he writes in the first chapter of *The City of God*, "for in the sack of the city they were an open sanctuary for all who fled to them, whether Christian or pagan."[7] Priest and historian Paulus Orosius, a contemporary of Augustine's, reports that Alaric explicitly told his soldiers not to trespass into churches: "If anyone fled into the basilicas of the holy apostles Peter and Paul, these, first of all, were to be granted security and inviolability."[8] Churches were respected as holy sanctuaries of protection.

In his book *Sanctuary and Crime in the Middle Ages, 400–1500*, Karl Shoemaker tracks the emergence of this tradition. Early in its history, church leaders turned to the biblical language of "intercession" from 1 Timothy 2 as a summons to the ecclesial vocation of sanctuary. According to their exegesis of the Pauline text, God had commissioned churches to intercede on behalf of fugitives from punishment. "I urge that supplications, prayers, intercession, and thanksgiving be made for everyone," the author of 1 Timothy writes (2:1). "For there is one God; there is also one mediator between God and humankind, Christ Jesus" (1 Tim. 2:5). And God has invited Christians to share in the intercessory work of Christ. "As early Christian theology raised intercession to the level of a divine attribute of Christ," Shoemaker explains, "intercession for sanctuary seekers became a defining task for bishops and saints alike."[9] Christ's role as intercessor was expected to be extended through the life of the church, his body in the world. For example, the Council of Serdica, convened in 343 CE, directed churches to intercede on behalf of people "who on account of their crimes have been sentenced [to punishment]."[10] The church was supposed to intercede because God has commissioned the body of Christ to intervene on behalf of fugitives. An intercessory Christology produced an ecclesiological posture of sanctuary.

This intercessory work of the church became the holy responsibility of churches early in the Middle Ages, according to Shoemaker. The bishops who gathered in Provence, France, for the Council of Orange in 441 CE, for instance, included in their canons the following decree: "If any one has taken refuge in a church he shall not be given up, but shall be sheltered from respect to the sacred place."[11] Congregations throughout the Roman Empire evidently followed the commands of the bishops since, in the sixth century when Emperor Justinian I updated the imperial laws, his *Code of Justinian* included a mandate to honor ecclesial sanctuary: "We ordain that no one be permitted to drag away those who have fled to sacrosanct churches."[12] This respect for congregational acts of sanctuary became the norm in European jurisprudence. In his *Decretum*, a compilation of canon laws, twelfth-century legal scholar Gratian distilled the sanctuary decrees from previous ecclesiastical councils into this dictum: "Concerning those who flee to church: they should not be dragged out, but defended by intercession and out of reverence for the sacred place."[13]

In the 1980s, here in the United States, churches experienced the rebirth of this tradition as a response to the Central American refugee crisis. At the time, under the auspices of anti-

communism, President Reagan was helping the oppressive regimes of right-wing leaders in Guatemala and El Salvador, whose
violent grasp on power resulted in masses of people escaping to
the north, across border after border, with nothing but hope for
survival. Reagan, however, did not welcome these refugees. He
did not want to admit to the public that the United States was involved in violences dreadful enough to cause thousands of people to flee their homes. He called them economic migrants, not
political refugees. Reagan refused to recognize them as asylees
from state repression, from the governments his administration
was funding and the death squads his military was training.
While US officials washed their hands of the crisis at the border,
churches decided to intercede on behalf of the refugees.[14]

"The sanctuary movement has arisen," Renny Golden and
Michael McConnell announced in 1986, "in a nation that trains
and arms the killers of innocent persons and then deems it criminal to shelter the victims of that slaughter."[15] Golden and Mc-
Connell were organizers in the US sanctuary movement from
the beginning in the early 1980s. They were especially involved
as "conductors" who would drive undocumented Central Americans from churches in the Southwest to safer locations in the
Midwest. Their book, *Sanctuary: The New Underground Railroad*, offers an insider's account of the networks and coalitions
across the continent that organized efforts to protect the lives of
Central Americans from deportation, which would've meant a
death sentence back home. In the mid-1980s, at its height, over
four hundred congregations had declared themselves part of the
movement, and roughly sixty thousand people were involved
in the work.[16] They provided sanctuary and accompaniment,
despite the Federal Bureau of Investigation's threats to charge
participants with felonies.

On March 24, 1982—the anniversary of Archbishop Óscar Romero's assassination[17]—at coordinated press conferences in Tucson, Arizona, and San Francisco, California, the first churches announced that they would house and protect refugees on their property, in defiance of the federal laws against harboring undocumented immigrants.[18] The church in Tucson—Southside Presbyterian Church—sent a letter to US Attorney General William French Smith II to inform the government of their act of civil disobedience. "We are writing to inform you that the Southside Presbyterian Church will publicly violate the Immigration and Nationality Act Section 274(a). We have declared our church as a 'sanctuary' for undocumented refugees from Central America."[19] The letter continues, "Obedience to God requires this of all of us."[20] That first year of the movement, the Southside congregation alone harbored sixteen hundred Central Americans on their way to homes and churches throughout the United States and Canada in what became known as a new underground railroad, a clandestine network of drivers and safe houses. As Rev. Jesse Jackson said in 1984 when his community in Chicago, Operation PUSH, welcomed a Salvadoran family into protective sanctuary, "We are going to create a network as great as the underground railroad that brought slaves to freedom more than one hundred years ago."[21] Their witness in the 1980s inspired ours during the Trump years.[22]

Church World Service, an ecumenical organization for refugees and immigrants in the United States, hired staff to facilitate communication among the people in sanctuary and to advocate on their behalf at the national level. Here in North Carolina, since we had the most people living in church sanctuary of all the states, we formed the NC Sanctuary Coalition as part of the NC Council of Churches to coordinate our efforts and amplify our witness. We were prepared for a movement, like in the 1980s, of Christian hospitality and solidarity with immigrants. And we expected that the sacrificial witness of the people in sanctuary—their perseverance and courage, their devotion to their families—would influence the political will of citizens toward compassion, perhaps even among the Christian voters who had been stalwart in their dedication to Trump's presidency. If our movement was overly optimistic about the public, we were not alone in our misjudgment.

In August 2018, Dave Eggers wrote a piece for the *New Yorker* about the contemporary rebirth of the sanctuary movement and the prospects for a shift toward a politics of solidarity with immigrants. He began his article with a quote from Studs Terkel: "There is a decency in the American people and a native intelligence—providing they have the facts, providing they have the information."[23] Eggers then provided information; he explained the situation of a Pakistani family of three who were living in protective sanctuary at a Congregational Church in Connecticut. After his heartfelt account of the family's story and the congregation's solidarity, he ended with a call for more churches to commit to offer sanctuary and for the public to turn against Trump's anti-immigrant policies. Our society will not be safer with more deportations, he concluded. "We will only be more callous, less compassionate, less fair, and we will continue to spin so far from the moral center that we may never find our way back."[24]

Our sanctuary movement did not have the political effects of the 1980s movement. At most we had nearly fifty churches, synagogues, and mosques involved in our solidarity work compared to their hundreds. In terms of a shift in political will, evangelical Christians doubled down with their support of Trump in his 2020 re-election campaign.[25] They wanted more of what he had to offer, even after his mass detention of immigrant children and his family separation policy. The valiant witness of several dozen people in church sanctuary would make little, if any, difference in such a calloused society.

In February 2020, after nearly two years of Rosa living at our church, the US Court of Appeals for the Fourth Circuit ruled in her favor. The three-judge panel unanimously overturned the immigration court's decision against Rosa and withdrew the government's order for her deportation.[26] "Me han garantizado mi libertad!" In her public statement, Rosa rejoiced with gratitude for her freedom to return to her children and community in Greensboro, North Carolina—to live without fear of arrest and deportation. "Pero recuerdo a todos mis amigos que aún luchan por su libertad, mis amigos que todavía están en santuario" (But I remember my friends who are striving for their freedom while still in sanctuary).

Rosa's victory has proven significant for other women who have sought asylum in the United States due to intimate-partner violence. In short, the court's ruling shifted the burden of proof to the government. In asylum cases, with respect to the United Nations' CAT, the government's attorney now must present evidence to refute the declarations of the applicant. "Once Rosa showed she suffered persecution the burden of proof shifted to the government," her attorney Ann Marie Dooley explained to *Religion News Service*.[27] "They didn't present any evidence that Rosa would no longer be in danger if she went back. The higher court said that was improper."[28] The decision shifted the burden of proof from asylum seekers to prove that they are still under threat to the government to prove that there is no longer a threat. Applicants like Rosa no longer have to provide evidence of ongoing persecution; instead, the government must prove that the persecution has ceased. In the Fourth Circuit Court decision, on behalf of the three-judge panel, Judge Diaz wrote that "the IJ [Immigration Judge] incorrectly placed the burden on [Rosa] Ortez-Cruz."[29] Instead, Judge Diaz explained, "The government must show that, if Ortez-Cruz relocates, it's more likely than not that Auceda [her abuser] won't threaten her for the rest of her life."[30] Without the government's attorney's evidence to the contrary, Judge Diaz made clear, "Ortez-Cruz has the benefit of the presumption."[31] In other words, with this federal court decision in Rosa's favor, survivors of abuse are now given the benefit of the doubt when they maintain that their abusers are still a threat.

This was her victory. She fought for her survival and won. *Ortez-Cruz v. Barr* is the name of the decision: her life in this country against US Attorney General William Barr's defense of President Trump's policies—and she won. She won her freedom, not only for herself and her children but for all the asylum seekers who are in similar situations, all the women who've fled from their abusers to safety in this country. With this legal precedent, she has reached out her hand to join them in the struggle for another chance at life.

"The first social ethical task of the church is to be the church—the servant community," the theologian Stanley Hauerwas has been reminding Christians since the 1980s.[32] "As such the church does not have a social ethic; the church is a social ethic."[33] We are our ethical vision. Our life with Rosa was an expression of who we are as a church, which was also a political proposal—a way of life that reorganizes how we understand our peoplehood, our belonging to one another.

For those years with her living in protective sanctuary, the ordinary habits of congregational life demonstrated an ecclesial politics that contrasted with the policies of the state. We organized our polis according the hospitality of the gospel, not according to the government's categories of citizen and alien, a division that renders some people deportable in order to protect the rights and privileges of others. The church is a diasporic people, which means we're always negotiating our political identity as a catholic body, a worldwide communion, despite the strictures of nation-states and their policed sectarianism.

- 7 -

LIBERATION FOR WORSHIP

In the late nineteenth century, Mexican Americans built houses in Chavez Ravine, a thirty-minute walk from downtown Los Angeles. Social forces of racial discrimination pushed them to the outskirts of the city. Over the next half century, immigrants from Mexico and Central America joined the community, which became a cluster of three neighborhoods: Bishop, Palo Verde, and La Loma. In the mid-twentieth century, as Los Angeles expanded, municipal authorities plotted to acquire the land with funding from the National Housing Act of 1949. Under the auspices of redevelopment, city authorities seized the property by eminent domain—promising that the residents would be allowed to return after the builders finished a public housing project.

Mayor Norris Poulson did not keep his city's promise to the inhabitants of Chavez Ravine. Instead of public housing, which he characterized as communist outposts—"creeping socialism"—Poulson negotiated the transfer of the land to the Dodgers franchise for a new stadium, to lure them from Brooklyn.[1]

"We've got to support and strengthen the downtown area," Poulson argued; "no city can be a great city without a strong central core."[2] With bulldozers behind them, the police invaded the neighborhoods and arrested whoever refused to leave their homes. The Los Angeles Dodgers had a new stadium in time for the 1962 season. The racism of urban planning displaced Mexican Americans, Chicanos, Mexicans, and Central and South American immigrants, relocating them to neighborhoods east and south of downtown.

These social forces directed my immigrant parents to a community tucked between industrial parks, in the long shadow cast by urban renewal. Our home was a quick drive from the plant where my dad worked, first as a janitor, then on the factory floor as a machinist. We made a life for ourselves at a safe distance from Mayor Poulson's cultural core, in an area of the city for people considered too brown for his visions of a luminous downtown. The city's social geography shoved us toward the manufacturing hub of the region, rendering my dad's labor more easily accessible to economic production—work befitting immigrants.

At the end of Genesis, socioeconomic forces pull the Hebrew people into ancient Egypt to survive the devastation of famine. The cries of hungry children compel them to migrate. At the direction of Pharaoh, the Hebrews settle in a region called Goshen, an area on the outskirts of the core of Egyptian life. "Goshen was quite near the frontier," Nahum M. Sarna explains in *Understanding Genesis*. This district was home to "a 'mixed multitude' [Exod. 12:38] of non-Egyptians" in "physical isolation from the mainstream of Egyptian life."[3] Pharaoh's imperial society was like the geography of Poulson's Los Angeles, with migrants dispersed to fringe real estate.

As the Hebrew men, the sons of Jacob, prepare for an audience with Pharaoh, their brother Joseph coaches them on how to respond to questions, how to stay out of trouble in this oppressive system he's learned to navigate over the decades of his assimilation. "When Pharaoh calls you and says, 'What is your occupation?' you shall say, 'Your servants have been keepers of livestock from our youth even until now'" (Gen. 46:33–34). They are to present themselves as useful subjects, as valuable to the economy, essential labor. Joseph also warns them to beware of a particular cultural reality: "All shepherds are abhorrent to the Egyptians" (Gen. 46:34). From their initial visit, a politics of abhorrence characterizes the reception of the Hebrews. They are invited to a feast but have to sit apart from the rest of the guests, at a segregated table—"because the Egyptians could not eat with the Hebrews, for that is an abomination to the Egyptians" (Gen. 43:32).

Despite the contemptuous gaze of the long-standing residents, the Hebrews make a home in this foreign land. They will do anything to keep their kids alive, even if this relocation will mean their constant subjection to their new neighbors' disgust.

After a while the factory where my dad worked moved the production line to a manufacturing compound in Tucson, Arizona, in search of cheaper labor. Our family had to follow the job. Immigrant lives serve the economy as precarious workers, available for relocation at the whims of a company's bottom line.

However, my parents soon discovered that, with the money from selling our house in California, we could afford to live in a much nicer neighborhood in Tucson—a location where people like us weren't supposed to own property. Instead of buying a house in South Tucson, close to the factories, my parents found a spot in the northern part of the city, near the foothills. The plant manager lived up the hill from our home, in the same development but above us, in a house with a view. Civilization has always built hierarchies into the environment.

The four of us—my mom, dad, sister, and I—were the only nonwhite people in the area. The neighbors had Lexus cars; we had an ocean-blue 1960s Volkswagen Bug, well used by previous owners. During weekends the car would be up on a ramp or jacks in our driveway so my dad could figure out how to fix a mechanical issue—whatever it took to keep the thing running. We did our own domestic work and our own yardwork. We hung our laundry on clotheslines in the backyard to dry. My dad never wore a shirt outside.

Since I moved away two decades ago, the demographics have shifted slightly. My parents were the advance guard of what euro-supremacists have called "the brown invasion"—a racial trope with a long history in the United States and now a political theme at home in the social vision of President Trump's Republican Party. "We cannot allow all of these people to invade our Country," President Trump wrote on Twitter in June 2018 about people crossing the southern border into the United States.[4] His attorney general used the same language a few months earlier, as if the two were passing around their party's handbook on nationalism. "We are not going to let this country be invaded. We will not be stampeded," Jeff Sessions said at a law-enforcement conference in Scottsdale, Arizona, a two-hour drive from my parents' house.[5]

In the biblical story, the abhorred Hebrews "swarmed and multiplied and grew very vast, and the land was filled with them"

(Exod. 1:7). Pharaoh and his people take stock of the demographic trends. These foreigners would become "more numerous and vaster than we," Pharaoh worries aloud at the data, "and then, should war occur, they will actually join our enemies and fight against us and go up from the land" (Exod. 1:9–10). Pharaoh's Egypt requires precarious Hebrew labor—workers who are indentured to the economy for their own livelihood yet whose personhood is considered alien to the cultural and political identity of the empire. Pharaoh needs them for the functioning of his society even though his fear converts their foreignness into a security threat.

"The overwhelming oppression is the collective fact that we do not fit," Gloria E. Anzaldúa writes of her Chicana identity in *La Prieta*, "and because we do not fit, we are a threat."[6] As Latiné peoples in the United States, we're like the Hebrews in Egypt—a threat to ethno-nationalists invested in their generational ascendency as preserved in the economic, political, and legal institutions that buttress our society. The election of Donald Trump was a last-ditch effort to consolidate that accumulated power. His administration responded to the demographic shift—our country becoming less white—with a wide-ranging policy of detention and deportation, and a protracted effort to refuse asylum applicants and deny refugees from Muslim-majority countries. Those federal directives cohered into a scattershot strategy to socially engineer a future for this country that wouldn't be so brown. Immigration policies are about social formation: about the making of a people, the construction of our collective identity. The political is personal, reaching into the intimacies of our friendships, of whom we belong to and who belongs to us—in our families, schools, neighborhoods, and religious communities.

The COVID-19 pandemic exposed US society as indebted to an economy of domination, a work structure that asserts a hierarchy of human value. In June 2020, an evening news segment on Univision featured fieldworkers in Florida who'd been told that they were essential to the food supply, yet had never been allowed a process to get legal permission to live in this country without fear of deportation. "Antes nos decían 'ilegales' y ahora somos 'esenciales'" (They used to call us "illegals," but now we're "essential"), Claudia González, an organizer with the Farmworker Association of Florida, told the reporter.[7] Legislators have set up a legal system that abhors the thought of residency permits for undocumented workers. Our economy demands their labor, while our politics detests their inclusion as citizens.

In his mid-twentieth-century report on the agricultural industry as the context to understand the immigrant experience in the United States, journalist Truman Moore titled his book *The Slaves We Rent*. "The migrant today is part of a system—Spanish in origin, and still tinged with the plantation way of life."[8] Moore investigated the dehumanizing conditions that had been produced by agribusiness in order to meet the economic demands for growth. "Without them—these two million men, women, and children who work the fields every year—the rise of American agriculture would not have been possible."[9]

Racialized social planning organizes domestic life, as my family experienced in Los Angeles and Tucson. But US power depends on segregation on an international scale—enforced by immigration policy and militarized borders—to produce a sense of peoplehood, to code individuals according to the laws of citizenship, which require that some are categorized as alien, as foreign, as migrant. The rights and privileges of every US citizen depend on maintaining a legal difference from others as aliens. Citizenship exists within geographies of confinement.

The US economy plunders wealth from the other side of borders while fencing out people desperate for the livelihood taken from them. Border security implements structures of confinement, rendering migrants as indentured servants to the global economy and pawns in the political schemes of superpowers. "Migrant and undocumented workers thus are the flip side of transnational capitalist outsourcing," Harsha Walia explains in *Undoing Border Imperialism*, "which itself requires border imperialism and racialized empire to create differential zones of labor."[10] The United States admits the flow of capital while regulating transnational demographics by excluding foreign bodies, renaming neighbors as enemies of the law, as threats to a way of life.

In *Migra! A History of the U.S. Border Patrol*, Kelly Lytle Hernández traces the development of a racial category for immigrants—"the migrant" from south of the border as a name for a particular racial identity, justifiably profiled by the immigration police according to US law. By means of the Border Patrol, Hernández writes in her epilogue, the federal government "imported the borderlands' deeply rooted racial divides arising from conquest and capitalist economic development into the making of US immigration law enforcement and, in turn, transformed the legal/illegal divide into a problem of race."[11] Border security, as required for the protection of citizenship rights, enforces segregation worldwide as some populations secure their power over others according to a hierarchy imposed through our globalized political economy. Gentrification on a global scale, as Fredric Jameson describes our crisis.[12]

Our global situation, where we live and work within political and economic arrangements that connect one part of the world with another, is a "patrón colonial de poder," in Aníbal Quijano's words—a colonial matrix pieced together as European powers enslaved peoples from the continent of Africa to use for civilization-building while also pursuing a genocidal exploitation of land and resources in the Americas.[13] This matrix of forces has configured our world for European powers—and their heirs in the Americas—to extract labor and resources from populations and geographies throughout the globe.[14]

The United States now harbors these forces that enlist our lives—as political and economic creatures whose well-being is bound up with the supremacy of our country—in the ongoing colonization of the earth. Military interventions and diplomatic negotiations work in conjunction with the business interests of conglomerates as they extract resources from the two-thirds world. In the Americas, the United States has indentured the economies of neighboring countries. "Latin America is the region of open veins," as Eduardo Galeano depicts the intra-American relationships:

> Everything, from the discovery until our times, has always been transmuted into European—or later United States—capital, and as such has accumulated in distant centers of power. Everything: the soil, its fruits and its mineral-rich depths, the people and their capacity to work and to consume, natural resources and human resources. Production methods and class structure have been successively determined from outside for each area by meshing it into the universal gearbox of capitalism. To each area has been assigned

a function, always for the benefit of the foreign metropolis of the moment, and the endless chain of dependency has been endlessly extended.[15]

The plantation economy has become the globalized economic system, operated by "mechanisms of plunder."[16]

Galeano's narrative in *Open Veins of Latin America* is a history of the present economic conditions of the Americas. His argument tracks the evolving forces of plunder—*despojo* in the original Spanish version of the book—unleashed by European societies on the cusp of the modern age. To conclude, as Galeano turned his focus to the 1970s, the era in which he wrote the book, he titled the final chapter "The Contemporary Structure of Plunder." The legacy of Europe's dual operations of enslavement and colonization is the plundering of peoples and lands. The two violences cohere in colonial America; the domination of people categorized as foreign and the theft of indigenous land are inseparable in his description of our world.

Galeano's geopolitical analysis from the vantage point of the Americas echoes African condemnations of colonial empires. In the late eighteenth century, Ghanaian abolitionist Ottobah Cugoano considered the European plunder of African peoples, and the destruction of indigenous civilizations of the Americas, as concomitant. Cugoano asserts that Europe's "foreign settlements and colonies were founded on murders and devastations, and that they have continued their depredations in cruel slavery and oppression to this day."[17] Settlers decimated indigenous populations. The "unjust and diabolical traffic of buying and selling, and of enslaving men," was a continuation of the "infernal wickedness" of the colonists' foundational devastation.[18] In his treatise against enslavement, Cugoano returns again and again to the violence against the native peoples of the Americas. He does not talk about one without the other. "The Spaniards began their settlements in the West Indies and America, by depredations of rapine, injustice, treachery, and murder, . . . and their principles and maxims in planting colonies have been adopted, in some measure, by every other nation in Europe," Cugoano explains.[19] According to his narrative, the kidnapping and enslavement of African peoples followed from "this guiltful method of colonization," which "led them on from one degree of barbarity and cruelty to another: for when they had destroyed, wasted and desolated the native inhabitants, and when many of their own people, enriched with plunder, had retired, or returned home to enjoy their ill-gotten wealth, other resources for men to labour and cultivate the ground, and such other laborious employments were wanted."[20]

The race to plunder the Americas for land and resources produced the desire to plunder the African continent for forced labor. Cugoano describes the competition among European powers as they subjected peoples on multiple continents in their violent lust for wealth:

The base traffic of kidnapping and stealing men was begun by the Portuguese on the coast of Africa, and as they found the benefit of it for their own wicked purposes, they soon went on to commit greater depredations. The Spaniards followed their infamous example, and the African slave-trade was thought most advantageous for them, to enable themselves to live in ease and affluence by the cruel subjection and slavery of others. The French and English, and some

other nations in Europe, as they founded settlements and
colonies in the West Indies, or in America, went on in the
same manner, and joined hand in hand with the Portuguese
and Spaniards, to rob and pillage Africa, as well as to waste
and desolate the inhabitants of the western continent.[21]

To summarize Cugoano, while borrowing Galeano's words: Colonialism transmuted the violent control of land and lives into
capital for European societies. "The plunderers abroad send
home their cash as fast as they can," as Cugoano characterizes
the transatlantic scheme of theft.[22] This chain of exploitation
and appropriation extends the past into the present, Galeano explains, describing the legacy of colonialism's expansion across
the landscape of modernity.[23]

   The appearance of colonialism in the Americas inaugurated
a violent remaking of the political and economic geography.[24]
And, all along the way, as "dreadful and shocking as it is to
think," Cugoano observes, this upheaval "has been established
by royal authority and is still supported and carried on under a
Christian government."[25] Imperial forces achieved their domin-
ion over people and land by means of a cataclysmic reordering
of the world, with Christianity as the spiritual overseer of the
pillage and plunder.

   The colonial demons they unleashed in the Americas still
possess this continent, where populations are stratified according to race and where immigration policies and border security
enforce our commitments to a segregated geography. Angela Y.
Davis observes that economic development and migration policies coordinate "the increasingly global strategy of dealing with
populations of people of color and immigrant populations from

the countries of the Global South as surplus populations, as disposable populations."[26]

In the biblical narrative, after the Hebrews experience generations of Egyptian exploitation, God empowers Moses to lead the people into freedom from bondage. And this movement toward liberation is a call to gather for worship. "When you bring the people out from Egypt," God says to Moses, "you shall worship God on this mountain" (Exod. 3:12). Then, in his audience with Pharaoh, Moses demands that the people be freed in order to assemble in the wilderness to celebrate a festival with God (Exod. 5:1).

The spiritual is political. Worship involves liberation. To congregate as God's people is to organize for freedom from exploitation. The Hebrews' liturgical festival is a protest against the conditions of enslavement. God, in the story of the exodus, gathers people for the sake of a life without exploitation.

To prepare ourselves for worship is to set our faces toward liberation. Festival celebrations and worship rituals are communal practices that organize individuals into a people. Liturgies are routines of belonging that create and maintain a community. Religious customs form us in a collective identity. Gustavo Gutiérrez, the great Peruvian theologian and Dominican priest, has called this kind of formation "a style of life."[27] In his classic, *We Drink from Our Own Wells: The Spiritual Journey of a People*, Gutiérrez describes our biblical faith as an invitation to join in a "collective venture . . . under the prior action of the God who liberates"—a lifelong journey for people who're breaking free from the chains of "exploitation and death."[28] To worship is to open ourselves to this God of life, in whose presence we learn that "to reject a fellow human," Gutiérrez explains, "is to reject God."[29] We cannot separate our life with God from our life with our neighbor. With one comes the other, because "Christianity is a message of life," and "to liberate is to give life."[30]

Citizenship, at its best, outlines the responsibilities each of us bears in creating a society together. The nation-state, at its best, claims for us a people with whom to develop structures of care for the well-being of all. The trouble, however, is that global politics has configured our citizenship into a kind of policed sectarianism. We're told to care about our own people, our fellow citizens, the rightful members of our country. As for those who, according to our legal frameworks and political definitions, happen to live on the wrong side of the citizen-or-alien divide? Well, they're deportable from our sphere of concern, banished from the reach of our sense of mutual responsibility. If our laws determine that our society does not belong to them, then we can absolve ourselves of our obligations as their neighbors. Because, according to this form of political imagination, the bonds of citizenship trump the biblical call to love our neighbors. The requirements of statecraft short-circuit our ethical deliberation. The presumptions of nationalism relieve us from our nagging feelings of care and concern for undocumented others. After all, the law is the law, a social contract to preserve who we are as a people.

Biblical faith is a style of life in which we relearn our relations; we reconfigure our lives to receive the presence of God in our relationships with our neighbors. That's the nature of worship: the rituals of collective life that organize a vision of belonging in which we recognize as idolatry any sociopolitical system that demands the sacrifice of another for the sake of self-preservation.

In this liberatory movement of worship, we are following the Hebrews out of ancient Egypt. Their story helps us retell our story as we attend to our lives with a new awareness. This scriptural account is a lens through which we notice with renewed vision the politics of where we are: we see and confront the Pharaohs of our world, we name the evils bound up in our social location, and we decry the categorization of certain populations as exploitable, as expendable, as deportable. Worship is how we, as Christians, gather before the God of the Hebrews in order to center our lives on God's redemption of the world. In this American wilderness, we assemble as people of God's Spirit whose power liberates us for a life of love—to pledge ourselves to the well-being of our neighbors, near and far, to give ourselves to a freedom that is bound up with theirs. "Until we are all free, we are none of us free," Emma Lazarus wrote in her declaration of Jewish solidarity in the late nineteenth century—a saying that Fannie Lou Hamer adapted for the civil rights movement: "Nobody's free until everybody's free."[31]

In the Bible story, God leads the Hebrews into freedom with a pillar of fire by night and a cloud during the day. "The Lord went in front of them" (Exod. 13:21)—the presence of God as the presence of liberation, in the cloud and fire. The people don't know the way; they can't see beyond the thick fog and column of flames. All they know is where they are: in the wilderness, at the edge of freedom, where they take one step at a time, together. According to Christian mystical traditions, the Spirit of God manifests as a cloud of unknowing, in the flashes of brilliant darkness—but here, in this story, the experience of God is not only personal but political: a multitude becoming a people on their way toward an undisclosed redemption. The mystics remind us of the promise that, even though we haven't yet developed a program for a politics of liberation, God is in our wandering. Here, in this US wilderness, the Spirit beckons a people to be reborn into the life of God's love for the world—for us to love our neighbors with the love of God and to proclaim our deliverance from the walls and policies that obstruct us from the fullness of life with our neighbors, citizens and noncitizens alike. A life of mutual care that corrodes barricades is the worshipful politics of God's liberation.

CONCLUSION

Migration, as a plotline to our human condition, has become a dominant feature of the story of our global community as a result of climate change. "Roughly two hundred million people globally live along coastlines less than five meters above today's sea level," observes Brian Fagan in his book *The Attacking Ocean: The Past, Present, and Future of Rising Sea Levels.*[1] "By the end of the twenty-first century, this figure is projected to increase to four hundred million," he continues.[2] Given the stubborn refusal of our political leaders to adjust the economies of the most powerful nation-states in order to avert our global environmental catastrophe, the seas will continue to rise. As the waters from melting glaciers and ice sheets erode coastlines inch by inch, the flooding of cityscapes and farmlands will exacerbate geopolitical crises in our century as multitudes are forced to migrate. Fagan predicts "a future of accelerating humanitarian crisis that may involve resettling millions of people in completely different rural and urban environments."[3] In his epilogue, Fagan hopes for intergovernmental partnership as

Western nation-states prepare to welcome immigrants: "The answer lies in levels of international cooperation and funding to handle migration unheard of in today's world."[4]

Christian Parenti is not as hopeful in the international cooperation of our governments to make the necessary changes. In *Tropic of Chaos: Climate Change and the New Geography of Violence*, Parenti describes the cataclysmic effects of climate change on the "economically and politically battered post-colonial states girding the planet's mid-latitudes"—that is, between the Tropic of Capricorn and the Tropic of Cancer.[5] We've instigated a global situation where people have to leave their homes and communities in order to survive as climate refugees. The US government has been preparing for the worldwide reordering of populations—preparing not to welcome survivors but to keep the hordes away. "The Pentagon is planning for a world remade by climate change," Parenti observes; "the Pentagon is planning for Armageddon."[6] Migrants, according to this plan, are not considered resourceful people, ready to contribute to society, but threats to the social order.

In a previously classified presentation to Congress, Thomas Fingar, the former deputy director of National Intelligence for Analysis, focused the legislators' attention on the effects of climate change and global migration patterns. "Extreme weather events and growing evidence of inundation will motivate many [people] to move sooner rather than later," Fingar explained.[7] "Closer to home, the United States will need to anticipate and plan for growing immigration pressures."[8]

Parenti documents the reports and analyses, like Fingar's, that have been shaping the conversation about climate change among our political leaders. A 2004 report commissioned by the Pentagon—"An Abrupt Climate Change Scenario and Its Implications for United States National Security"—paints an ominous picture of the future, "as famine, disease, and weather-related disasters strike due to the abrupt climate change." The report continues: "Nations with the resources to do so may build virtual fortresses around their countries, preserving resources for themselves."[9] According to Parenti, "national security intellectuals, in and out of government, have started to imagine a militarized geography of social breakdown on a global scale."[10] He names this grand plan for the emerging global migration crisis "climate fascism"—a politics of "exclusion, segregation, and repression," a strategy of "walls, guns, barbed wire, armed aerial drones, [and] permanently deployed mercenaries."[11] Wealthy and powerful nation-states, like the United States, are preparing themselves to be an "armed lifeboat," a kind of Noah's ark, but one that deploys surveillance drones instead of doves.[12]

Noah's ark, outfitted as an armed lifeboat, seems like an appropriate image for our response to the catastrophe of global warming. With militarized border fences patrolled by drones, leaders in the United States are constructing for us a country that will attempt to float above the waves, untouched by the lives at the border. In *State of Disaster: The Failure of U.S. Migration Policy in an Age of Climate Change*, Maria Cristina Garcia documents how climate disasters in our region of the world have displaced people from their homelands, forcing them to seek refuge in countries that have amassed enough wealth to subsidize a society's perseverance through cycles of ecological cataclysms. The chaos of extreme weather events, of floods and droughts, decimates all kinds of communities—but these disasters and their aftermath are especially devastating among populations in environments that, over the long history of economic exploitation and extraction, have been plundered of resources. Garcia refers to findings from climate demography that estimate a yearly average of 1.5 million refugees from Mexico and Central America at the US border due to food insecurity by 2050.[13] This is the outlook if we don't drastically reduce our production of greenhouse gasses, while also doing our part to restore agricultural networks throughout the Americas.

However, our leaders here in the United States have instead chosen to fortify our borders, transforming our society into a walled fortress. "Anticipating conflict in a world of accelerating climate change," Garcia observes, "nations are responding with greater militarization, the surveillance of populations, and the repression of civil liberties and civil rights to protect and maintain control over resources, supply chains, and private property."[14] Rather than organizing our lives according to the possibilities of a sanctuary politics, our leaders have opted for what Parenti calls climate fascism. Without political pressure to reorient the course of our national politics in relation to our neighbors, the bipartisan leadership in our government will content themselves with the momentum of our anti-immigrant policies and continue to invest in the most advanced military technologies as ramparts for the border. And we will be grateful for our jobs and community gardens—a society protected from the chaos beyond the walls.

Recent intergovernmental policies and transnational policing have attempted to push the evidence of our global migration crisis farther south into Central America, as far as possible from our lives. Beginning with the Mérida Initiative in 2008, then the Programa Frontera Sur in 2014, the United States has funded and developed immigration enforcement infrastructure throughout Mexico to quell migration—militarized checkpoints and patrols to dam the flow of people before they reach the US border.[15] Yet these strategic designs for migration management have succeeded only in further imperiling those on the journey—shifting migrant trails into more dangerous terrain, empowering federal police throughout Mexico to abuse migrants with impunity, and fueling the indiscriminate violence of drug cartels as they fight for control over routes for human smuggling.[16] If history offers any revelations about human ingenuity and tenacity for survival, we should know by now that we can't stop ourselves from doing what we have to do in order to live—and to care for others along the way as we share in the travails of the human condition.

While volunteering at La Casa del Migrante in Tijuana, Mexico, I met a woman who had recently arrived from Guatemala. She was pregnant, within weeks of her due date, she told me one evening in the best Spanish she could put together. She was from a Mayan community in the mountains, and Spanish was probably her third or fourth language, which was all she needed for the task at hand. We were chatting while sorting through piles of clothes. I was on *ropa* duty that day, which meant that after the community meal, I would unlock the storage room with all the donated clothing, and residents of the shelter would line up for an opportunity to pick out new pants, a shirt, a jacket, socks and underwear, shoes—whatever was available, whatever they needed.

She really needed a new pair of shoes, she said. I walked her over to the shelves and rummaged through the stacks to find a decent pair in her size. As we poked around at the options, which weren't ideal, she glanced over at a huge stash of shoes on the floor and chuckled to herself. I looked over and laughed too. The mound in the corner was made up of high heels—stilettos and platform shoes. She asked me if anyone picks from those, and I told her that no one ever does, which is why the pile just gets bigger and bigger. Then I tried to explain the cultural phenomenon called "Southern California," and how all the donations came from nice people in wealthy neighborhoods in Los Angeles and San Diego, and how I guess they hadn't quite thought through what it's like to try to walk through the desert, to cross the border, in stilettos. We both shrugged and laughed as I handed her a pair of very reasonable Nikes that looked like they might fit.

Later that evening a long-term volunteer at the shelter stopped by the *cuarto de ropa* and asked if I could pick out some baby outfits. She'd decided that the shelter should throw a baby shower for the soon-to-be mom. So I stayed late that evening, sorting through boxes of clothes, picking out the cutest onesies and newborn outfits, and pondered how the world has come to be the way it is, where the best option some people have for survival is to leave their ancestral land, their community, their family, and risk everything at the border.

The next day, as we gathered for morning prayer, our cohort of volunteers, the eight of us, decided to pitch in some cash to buy a cake and party supplies for the grandest baby shower celebration the migrant shelter has ever seen. We passed around a basket as the priest led us through the morning liturgy, which concluded with a lively rendition of Leonard Cohen's "Hallelujah." I'm not sure if, before this moment, I would've considered the song appropriate for prayer; but, somehow, a month before I arrived, a volunteer had convinced the young priest from Vietnam—who, mind you, hadn't at that point in his ministry needed to learn English—that Cohen's song was appropriate to sing as a kind of benediction.

The priest took out his guitar (he'd learned the tune at the volunteer's request), and we had a Leonard Cohen sing-along as we held hands and swayed. Even though the priest didn't know all the words, he led us as we offered to God our broken hallelujahs.

That night there was a party, with all the newly arrived guests gathered to offer gifts to a woman they'd never met before, as she prepared to welcome a child in the shadow of a society that couldn't care less about her life or the life of her child. But there, in Tijuana, among strangers from everywhere, from Syria to Nigeria, from Brazil to Ecuador—there, in that shelter, the community celebrated with balloons and streamers, cupcakes and hot chocolate, music and dancing.

A couple weeks later, after I'd returned to North Carolina, a friend from the shelter texted me pictures of the newborn. She let me know that the mother and infant were healthy. The lead priest of the shelter was committed to letting them stay for as long as needed, until she was ready to try to cross the border again, this time with a baby.

That world at the border is not far from the world into which Jesus was born, with Mary and Joseph on their own, far away from their community, in an abandoned corner of society, alone, except for the strangers who showed up to celebrate. At that first-century baby shower, the shepherds from the fields offered the only gifts they had: words, the words from the angels they had seen in the fields, the promises of God, news of hope. And "Mary treasured all these words and pondered them in her heart," the Scriptures tell us (Luke 2:19).

With the shepherds and animals gathered around her child, Mary received their words as treasures and kept them in her heart for safekeeping, to be there for her when she would need them again, when she'd need the strength of God's promises for her plight.

There is much to wonder about, so much to ponder—about what has happened to us and what has happened to our world. Lives devastated as a result of immigration policies and enforcement. Family members torn from each other. The pounding dread that today will be the day of their arrest and deportation. A weaponized environment, orchestrating death in the borderlands. There is a political wound at the heart of how we organize ourselves as a country. There are people like Mary at every juncture in our body politic, where the border between citizen and alien cuts into our common life.

There are people like the woman in that Tijuana shelter, hoping for a better world for her teenager; and Rosa, living in a church, waiting for the promise of a life with her children. People like Mary—bewildered and exhausted, searching for words to treasure, to hold on to, signs of a world about to turn, daybreak to end the nightmares.

And, in the meantime, people invent reasons for joy in the face of despair. Like the detainees at the Eloy facility who pool their meager resources to buy overpriced Doritos and "pork product" as ingredients for their creative attempt at a Christmas feast of tamales.

Despite it all, there are people who get together to make hope possible. There are baby showers in migrant shelters and people who look out for each other and strangers who do what they can with what they have—to celebrate life in the midst of violence, to prophesy the dawning of a new day even while walking through valleys shadowed with death.

There are always good reasons to sing a hallelujah, even if our hope falters, even if we're overwhelmed at the realities of our wounded world, overcome at the devastation—to sing a broken hallelujah on behalf of a broken world. Because we believe that our neighbors—regardless of citizenship status, residency documentation, or whether they live on this side or the other side of the border—are held in God's care. The Bible reminds us that God has been known to join caravans in the wilderness. The Spirit of God dwells with people on the move. A migrant God for migrant life.

To believe in this God is to live with hope, to depend on and lean toward hope, to entrust our hope to the transforming power of the Holy Spirit—the Spirit who invites us to pray, with Jesus, for God to remake our earthly lives according to the image of heavenly life. "Thy kingdom come" (Matt. 6:10). Our spiritual longing is also a political longing. To pray for the transfiguration of our earthly politics is to open ourselves toward God's promises—for hope to come alive in our collective struggle as we ready ourselves for a new world.

ACKNOWLEDGMENTS

This book began as a sermon I preached at my church in 2011. I'm grateful for Chapel Hill Mennonite for teaching me how to preach, and to think and write. They've been my first and primary context for working out my theology over almost two decades.

That sermon more than a decade ago about a migrant God turned into a conversation with my friend Jonathan Wilson-Hartgrove, which became a disagreement we sorted out in print, thanks to *Sojourners Magazine*: "Stability vs. Mobility," *Sojourners* (July 2012). Another friend, Lauren Winner, encouraged me to keep on thinking on this theme, first by offering invitations to speak to her class at Duke Divinity School, then by her gentle prodding as she kept asking me how the book was coming along. She helped my ideas take the shape of a book.

Another beginning for this book was my parents' migration stories and our family life in California and Arizona. Growing up in the United States, I couldn't help but think about my own life as stretching south of the border, given my relationships with grandparents, aunts and uncles, and cousins living mostly in three American countries (the United States, Costa Rica, and Colombia). With these familial ties reaching across borders, I've always had a transnational sense of belonging. I'm grateful for my extended family for welcoming me, whenever I visit, as if I am returning home. Their love, even from afar, has made me who I am.

My parents, Cecilia Salas Villegas and Ruben Villegas Estrada, have given so much of themselves to make my life possible, including all the sacrifices involved in providing an education for me. The ability to write this book is a testimony to their love and care and provision. I've relied on the love and friendship of my sister, Cynthia, as we keep on sorting through our lives. My wife, Katie, has lovingly encouraged me in my vocational twists and turns, as we've made a life together in which we've both been able to pursue our gifts and callings.

The material in this book incorporates a decade of pastoral ministry and community activism, which I have written about along the way. Below is a list of articles that have been reworked and incorporated into this book. I'm grateful for permission to include them in these pages. "When Death in the Desert Is Not an Accident" (*Sojourners*, June 2019, www.sojo.net) is incorporated in chapter 1; "A Liturgy in the Borderlands" © 2022 by the *Christian Century* is excerpted by permission from the October 2022 issue of the *Christian Century* in chapter 2; "The Kindom of Mi Abuelita" (*Mennonite*, March 27, 2015) and "Worship with God's Pueblo" (*Mennonite Weekly Review*, June 21, 2010) are incorporated in chapter 3; "At Tijuana Shelter Casa del Migrante, Every Meal Is Holy" © 2017 by the *Christian Century* is excerpted by permission from the November 17, 2021, issue of the *Christian Century* in chapter 3; "Lamenting with My Jewish Neighbors on Tisha B'Av" © 2020 by the *Christian Century* is excerpted by permission from the April 8, 2020, issue of the *Christian Century* in chapter 4; "Immigration Law and the Politics of Disgust" © 2020 by the *Christian Century* is excerpted by permission from the December 16, 2020, issue of the *Christian Century* in chapter 7; and "A Shower in the Desert" © 2022 by the *Christian Century* is excerpted by permission from the December 2022 issue of the *Christian Century* in my conclusion. As is clear from the list, I thought through a lot of my early ideas in the pages of the *Christian Century* magazine, where I've worked with Steve Thorngate. He's a gifted editor, and I've been grateful for his careful attention to my writing. At *Sojourners* I worked with Betsy Shirly, at *Mennonite Weekly Review* I worked with Paul Schrag, and at the *Mennonite* I worked with Hannah Heizenker. I'm grateful to each of them for their insights and suggestions. In these last stages of writing, several friends were generous with their time in reading drafts of chapters: Ali Aslam, Peter Dula, Melissa Florer-Bixler, Xaris A. Martínez, Jed Purdy, and Scott Schomburg. A team of editors helped turn my drafts into a book: Lisa Ann Cockrel and Laurel Draper at Eerdmans, and Erika Harman. Thanks for your careful work.

A pastoral study grant from the Louisville Institute made possible the research travel for this book project; I'm grateful to have worked with Edwin Aponte, Don Richter, and Keri Liechty as part of the grant. I wrote first drafts of two chapters while at the Collegeville Institute for a writing residency; I'm grateful for the leadership of Jacqueline Bussie and the organizational care of Carla Durand.

This book is about courageous and inspiring people. It's been a privilege to have met them along my wandering path, and I'm grateful to them for letting me include parts of their stories in this book. I've written about them because they've become part of my sense of belonging—of what it means to make this country my home, with them.

NOTES

INTRODUCTION

1. "En Dios ponemos la confianza, Salmo 36," in *Una luz en el camino: Oraciones, salmos, cánticos y una guía para migrantes y peregrinos,* ed. Casa del Migrante, Tecún Umán (Antigua Guatemala: Copia Fiel, 2013), 17. Translations are my own.

2. Frances Stonor Saunders, "Where on Earth Are You?," *London Review of Books* 38, no. 5 (March 3, 2016), http://tinyurl.com/bdh32vkw.

3. Saunders, "Where on Earth Are You?"

4. Saunders, "Where on Earth Are You?"

5. Saunders, "Where on Earth Are You?"

6. Saunders, "Where on Earth Are You?" Saunders quotes from Mattathias Schwartz, "The Anchor," *New Yorker*, April 21, 2014, http://tinyurl.com/2t49cvb5.

7. Missing Migrants Project, "Mediterranean," International Organization for Migration, http://tinyurl.com/3sjkcwxa.

8. Dorothee Sölle, *The Mystery of Death* (Minneapolis: Fortress, 2007), 112.

9. For accounts of Samuel's arrest and deportation, see Barry Yeoman, "ICE Puts Immigrants into a Cruel Catch-22," *Nation*, December 6, 2018, http://tinyurl.com/ycxc52y8. And Pilar Timpane, "After Samuel Oliver-Bruno's Deportation, a Sanctuary Community Suffers Together," *Sojourners Magazine*, December 3, 2018, http://tinyurl.com/3ctw6y8d.

10. Peter C. Phan outlines a theological framework for this claim: Phan, "*Deus Migrator*—God the Migrant: Migration of Theology and Theology of Migration," *Theological Studies 77*, no. 4 (December 2016): 845–68.

CHAPTER 1

1. Brady McCombs, "Rain Washes Away 40 Feet of US-Mexico Border Fence," *Arizona Daily Star*, August 10, 2011, http://tinyurl.com/5f6u8et6.

2. Hope Reese, "He Was a Border Patrol Agent. What He Saw Gave Him Nightmares," *Vox*, February 15, 2018, http://tinyurl.com/ynjhduvu.

3. Francisco Cantú, *The Line Becomes a River: Dispatches from the Border* (New York: Riverhead Books, 2018), 33.

4. La Coalición de Derechos Humanos and No More Deaths, "Death & Disappearance on the U.S.-Mexico Border," part 2, page 1, http://tinyurl.com/kckdn2a9.

5. US Border Patrol, *Border Patrol Strategic Plan 1994 and Beyond: National Strategy*, (July 1994), pp. 7, 10, Homeland Security Digital Library, http://tinyurl.com/2a9kmyct.

6. Jason Mark, "The Border Patrol Has Turned the Desert Wilderness into a Lethal Weapon," *Sierra*, August 22, 2017, http://tinyurl.com/4svptuc6.

7. La Coalición de Derechos Humanos and No More Deaths, *Death & Disappearance on the U.S.-Mexico Border*, part 2, Interference with Humanitarian Aid (n.p.: n.d.), 4, http://tinyurl.com/kckdn2a9.

8. Joseph Nevins, *Operation Gatekeeper and Beyond: The War on "Illegals" and the Remaking of the U.S.-Mexico Boundary*, 2nd ed. (New York: Routledge, 2010), 174. I'm grateful to Robin Reineke for recommending this book to me.

9. Nevins, *Operation Gatekeeper and Beyond*, 205.

10. "US-Mexico Border World's Deadliest Migration Land Route," The International Organization of Migration, September 12, 2023, http://tinyurl.com/3n855maw.

11. U.S. Government Accountability Office, *Southwest Border: CBP Should Improve Data Collection, Reporting, and Evaluation for the Missing Migrant Program*, by Rebecca Gambler, GAO-22-105053, Washington, DC: April 20, 2022, GAO, http://tinyurl.com/2stsk3w2.

12. Robin Reineke, "Necroviolence and Postmortem Care along the U.S.-México Border," in *The Border and Its Bodies: The Embodiment of Risk along the U.S.-México Line*, ed. Thomas E. Sheridan and Randall H. McGuire (Tucson: University of Arizona Press, 2019), 154.

13. Reineke, "Necroviolence and Postmortem Care," 158.

14. See Seth Schermerhorn, *Walking to Magdalena: Personhood and Place in Tohono O'odham Songs, Sticks, and Stories* (Lincoln: University of Nebraska Press, 2019), 39, 147–48.

15. Stephen Lemons, "Blood's Thicker Than Water," *Phoenix New Times*, February 25, 2010, http://tinyurl.com/2xftyj98.

16. José Antonio Lucero, "Friction, Conversion, and Contention: Prophetic Politics in the Tohono O'odham Borderlands," *Latin American Research Review*, vol. 49 (2014): 168–84. For further exploration of Mike Wilson's life and work, see José Antonio Lucero and Mike Wilson, *What Side Are You On? A Tohono O'odham Life across Borders* (Chapel Hill: University of North Carolina Press, 2024).

17. Kelly Lytle Hernández, *Migra! A History of the U.S. Border Patrol* (Berkeley: University of California Press, 2010), 132.

18. Hernández, *Migra!*, 132.

19. Hernández, *Migra!*, 132.

20. Hernández, *Migra!*, 132.

21. Hernández, *Migra!*, 229.

22. See Ignacio Ellacuría, "El pueblo crucificado, ensayo de soteriología histórica," in *Conversión de la Iglesia al Reino de Dios para anunciarlo y realizarlo en la historia* (San Salvador, El Salvador: UCA Editores, 1985), 25-63.

23. Jon Sobrino, *Jesus the Liberator: A Historical-Theological Reading of Jesus of Nazareth* (Maryknoll, NY: Orbis, 1993), 195-96.

24. For the language of "social death," I'm indebted to Orlando Patterson, *Slavery and Social Death: A Comparative Study*, 2nd ed. (Cambridge, MA: Harvard University Press, 2018). Angela Y. Davis has argued that we should consider the prison within the genealogy of enslavement and the plantation economy in the United States. See Davis, "From the Prison of Slavery to the Slavery of Prison: Frederick Douglass and the Convict Lease System," and "Racialized Punishment and Prison Abolition," in *The Angela Y. Davis Reader*, ed. Joy James (Oxford: Blackwell, 1998).

25. Caleb Smith, *The Prison and the American Imagination* (New Haven, CT: Yale University Press, 2009), 39.

26. Harry Hawser, quoted in Caleb Smith, *Prison and the American Imagination*, 27.

27. Charles Dickens, *American Notes* (New York: Penguin, 2000), 113; quoted in Smith, *Prison and the American Imagination*, 38.

28. George Jackson, *Soledad Brother: The Prison Letters of George Jackson* (Chicago: Lawrence Hill Books, 1994), 14, 63; quoted in Smith, *Prison and the American Imagination*, 27.

29. Jimmy Santiago Baca, *A Place to Stand* (New York: Grove, 2001), 117; quoted in Smith, *Prison and the American Imagination*, 193.

30. Ignacio Ellacuría, "The Latin American Quincentenary: Discovery or Cover-up?," in *Ignacio Ellacuría: Essays on History, Liberation, and Salvation*, ed. Michael E. Lee (Maryknoll, NY: Orbis, 2013), 34.

31. After my visit, I found the names of the three people who died by suicide: Elsa Guadalupe Gonzales was twenty-four years old, Jorge Garcia Maldanado was forty, and Jose De Jesus Deniz Sahagun was thirty-one. Freedom for Immigrants maintains data on US detention center populations: https://www.freedomforimmigrants.org/map.

In their research into the suicide reports from immigrant detention facilities, Beatriz Aldana Marquez et al. argue that "the U.S. immigrant apparatus is a racial project that jeopardizes immigrants' wellbeing through organized failure" (1). They describe a system of "processing and detention riddled with impediments to their [detainees'] wellbeing, which ultimately pushes detainees to the edge, to poor mental health, and suicidality" (1). Beatriz Aldana Marquez et al., "Pushing Them to the Edge: Suicide in Immigrant Detention Centers as a Product of Organizational Failure," *Social Science & Medicine* 283 (August 2021): 114177, https://doi.org/10.1016/j.socscimed.2021.114177.

CHAPTER 2

1. Elizabeth F. Cohen, *Illegal: How America's Lawless Immigration Regime Threatens Us All* (New York: Basic Books, 2020), 49.

2. Cohen, *Illegal*, 47.

3. See the entries for λειτουργέω and λειτουργία in Fredrick W. Danker, Walter Bauer, William F. Arndt, and F. Wilbur Gingrich,

Greek-English Lexicon of the New Testament and Other Early Christian Literature, 3rd ed. (Chicago: University of Chicago Press, 2000), 590–91.

4. Bonnie Honig, *Antigone, Interrupted* (Cambridge, UK: Cambridge University Press, 2013), 7. I'm grateful to Ali Aslam for recommending Honig's book to me. Also see Martin Donougho, "The Woman in White: On the Reception of Hegel's *Antigone*," *Owl of Minerva*, vol. 21, no. 1 (Fall 1989): 65–89.

5. In chap. 6 of *Antigone, Interrupted*, Honig reads the play as a conspiracy between Antigone and Ismene to defy Creon's decree. "The sisters care for each other in turn: each guesses at the other's sacrifice in quiet isolation, and each utters the lines and performs the acts that both suit and extend her character." Honig, *Antigone, Interrupted*, 170.

6. Sophocles, *Antigone* in *The Three Theban Plays: Antigone, Oedipus the King, Oedipus at Colonus*, 32–36; trans. Robert Fagles (New York: Penguin, 1984), 60.

7. Sophocles, *Antigone*, 88–90; trans. Fagles, 63.

8. Sophocles, *Antigone*, 80–81; trans. Fagles, 62.

9. Sophocles, *Antigone*, 489–90; trans. Fagles, 81.

10. Karl Barth, *Church Dogmatics* II/2: 363, from Karl Barth, *Church Dogmatics*, 4 vols. (Edinburgh: T&T Clark, 1956–1975).

11. Karl Barth, *Church Dogmatics* II/1: 386, from Karl Barth, *Church Dogmatics*, 4 vols. (Edinburgh: T&T Clark, 1956–1975). For an account of Barth's politics of election, see chapter 7 of *Karl Barth and Radical Politics*, ed. George Hunsinger, 2nd ed. (Eugene, OR: Cascade, 2017): Hunsinger, "Toward a Radical Barth."

12. Honig, *Antigone, Interrupted*, 95.

13. Honig, *Antigone, Interrupted*, 194.

14. Sophocles, *Antigone*, 471–79; trans. Fagles, 80.

15. Honig, *Antigone, Interrupted*, 119.

16. For an account of communion as an act of hope for redemption, see Geoffrey Wainwright's *Eucharist and Eschatology* (New York: Oxford University Press, 1981).

17. See "The Church, Christians, and the Dead: Commemoration of the Dead in Late Antiquity," chap. 7 in Éric Rebillard, *The Care of the Dead in Late Antiquity*, trans. Elizabeth Trapnell Rawlings and Jeanine Routier-Pucci (Ithaca: Cornell University Press, 2009).

18. *Didascalia apostolorum*, 6.22.2-3; trans. Alistair Stewart-Sykes, *The* Didascalia Apostolorum: *An English Version with Introduction and Annotation* (Turnhout: Brepols, 2009), 255-56. For Stewart-Sykes's discussion on this passage, see pp. 79-80.

19. Johann Baptist Metz, *Faith in History and Society: Toward a Practical Fundamental Theology*, trans. David Smith (New York: Seabury, 1980). Bruce T. Morrill offers a helpful account of Metz's contribution to liturgical studies. Morrill, *Anamnesis as Dangerous Memory: Political and Liturgical Theology in Dialogue* (Collegeville, MN: Liturgical Press, 2000).

20. Sophocles, *Antigone*, 316; trans. Fagles, 72.

CHAPTER 3

1. Ada María Isasi-Díaz, *Mujerista Theology: A Theology for the Twenty-First Century* (Maryknoll, NY: Orbis, 1996). See her chap. 7, "Elements of a *Mujerista* Anthropology," 128-47. See also Isasi-Díaz, "Kin-dom of God: A Mujerista Proposal," in *In Our Own Voices: Latino/a Renditions of Theology*, ed. Benjamín Valentín (Maryknoll, NY: Orbis, 2010), 171-89.

2. Ada María Isasi-Díaz, *En la lucha (In the Struggle): Elaborating a Mujerista Theology* (Minneapolis: Fortress, 2004), 53.

3. Isasi-Díaz, *En la lucha*, 53.

4. Congregation of the Missionaries of St. Charles (Scalabrin-

ians), *Rules of Life* (Rome, 1999), n. 5; quoted in Giovanni Graziano Tassello, "For the Love of Migrants: The Scalabrinian Tradition," in *A Promised Land, A Perilous Journey: Theological Perspectives on Migration*, ed. Daniel G. Groody and Gioacchino Campese (Notre Dame, IN: University of Notre Dame Press, 2008), 135.

5. Patrick Murphy, CS, "Revolution of the Heart: Assisting Migrants in Their Quest for Dignity," in *Mobilizing Public Sociology: Scholars, Activists, and Latin@ Migrants Converse on Common Ground*, ed. Victoria Carty and Rafael Luévano (Boston, MA: Brill, 2017), 141.

6. Aristotle, *De partibus animalium*, 5.645a15–23; quoted in Martha Nussbaum, *The Fragility of Goodness: Luck and Ethics in Greek Tragedy and Philosophy*, 2nd ed. (New York: Cambridge University Press, 2001), 262.

CHAPTER 4

1. Bob Geary, "Zebulon Cops Targeting Latinos as They Go to Church," *IndyWeek*, April 29, 2010, http://tinyurl.com/3jmrcmtn.

2. Sarah Ovaska-Few, "Immigration Raids in Carey," *NC Newsline*, November 30, 2010, http://tinyurl.com/2jnpmkmw.

3. "Delegation of Immigration Authority Section 287(g) Immigration and Nationality Act," US Immigration and Customs Enforcement, updated January 3, 2024, https://www.ice.gov/identify-and-arrest/287g.

4. Mai Thi Nguyen and Hannah Gill, *The 287(g) Program: The Costs and Consequences of Local Immigration Enforcement in North Carolina Communities*, The Latino Migration Project at The University of North Carolina at Chapel Hill (Chapel Hill: University of North Carolina at Chapel Hill, 2010), v: http://tinyurl.com/3ta84cwh.

5. Nguyen and Gill, *The 287(g) Program*, 1.

6. Felicia Arriaga offers a comprehensive analysis of ICE's involvement in North Carolina, as well as community-organized efforts to unlink county participation in federal "crimmigration" policies. Felicia Arriaga, *Behind Crimmigration: ICE, Law Enforcement, and Resistance in America* (Chapel Hill: University of North Carolina Press, 2023). As she notes, "Between 2006 and 2008, places like North Carolina became the testing ground for various immigration enforcement practices meant to target the increase of mostly Latinx immigrants" (4).

7. Jacqueline Stevens, "America's Secret ICE Castles," *Nation*, December 16, 2009, http://tinyurl.com/3dzhkuse.

8. Stevens, "America's Secret ICE Castles."

9. James Pendergraph, as quoted in Stevens, "America's Secret ICE Castles."

10. "Liberating God, Your Son Taught Us to Pray," in *Hymnal: A Worship Book* (Scottdale, PA: Herald Press, 1992), no. 732.

11. Our litany was inspired by the "Litany of Resistance" from Shane Claiborne and Chris Haw, *Jesus for President: Politics for Ordinary Radicals* (Grand Rapids: Zondervan, 2008). See their appendix 4.

12. For news coverage of our Holy Thursday worship protest, see Yonat Shimron, "Dozens Protest at Jail for Aliens," *News & Observer* (Raleigh, NC), April 3, 2010.

13. See "Immigrant & Refugee Justice," Carolina Jews for Justice, updated 2022, http://tinyurl.com/59ryaetd.

14. See https://mijente.net/ and https://www.siembranc.org/.

15. See Bend the Arc's press release, which highlighted Jewish involvement in the demonstration: http://tinyurl.com/yeyk5bb3. For further coverage of the event, and the reasons for the protest, see Max Rivlin-Nadler, "Immigrants and Activists Flood San Diego to

Protest Operation Streamline," *Appeal*, July 6, 2018: http://tinyurl. com/wkvp9p67.

16. Roxana Bendezú and Brandon Mond, "Never Again, for Anyone," *Burlington Times-News*, November 22, 2019, http://tinyurl. com/mr4yfur9. For news coverage of the event, see Tina Vasquez, "American Jews Say 'Never Again' to Detainment of Immigrants," *Yes! Solutions Journalism*, December 2, 2019, http://tinyurl.com/ mtznk6kc. For the national context of the movement, see Ben Kesslan, "'Never Again Means Close the Camps': Jews Protest ICE across the Country," *NBC News*, July 15, 2019, http://tinyurl.com/ ye23sf55.

17. See the home page of Never Again Action, https://www.nev eragainaction.com/.

18. Ellen F. Davis, *Opening Israel's Scriptures* (New York: Oxford University Press, 2019), 291, 293.

19. Tamar Fox, "A Prayer for Undocumented Families Torn Apart," Ritualwell, 2018, http://tinyurl.com/38xbys8n.

20. Havah Eshel, "Tisha B'Av," *Reconstructionist* 51, no. 8 (July–August 1986): 7, stanza 5, lines 27–32. Used by permission.

CHAPTER 5

1. Teo Armus, "'New Normal' as 200 NC Immigrants Arrested," *Charlotte Observer*, February 9, 2019, 1A.

2. Joe Marusak and Cristina Bolling, "ICE Blasts New Sheriff for Ending Program," *Charlotte Observer*, December 8, 2018, 1A.

3. 287(g) is a federal policy agreement that formalizes the co-operation of local law enforcement with ICE. See my discussion in chapter 4.

4. Marusak and Bolling, "ICE Blasts New Sheriff," 1A.

5. Armus, "'New Normal,'" 1A.

6. Kelly Lytle Hernández, "America's Mass Deportation System Is Rooted in Racism," *Conversation*, February 26, 2017, http://tinyurl.com/3jrx6twv.

7. Durham City Council Meeting, November 15, 2010, agenda item 19, "Durham Bill of Rights Defense Committee and the Durham Immigrant Solidarity Committee." Listen to city council comments that begin at 1:33:35. http://tinyurl.com/yzkvtsvy.

8. Dawn Baumgartner Vaughn, "7 NC Mayors: ICE Raids Have Terrorized Communities," *Charlotte Observer*, February 17, 2019, 14A.

9. Board of County Commissioners, Durham, North Carolina. Minutes from the regular session on February 11, 2019. http://tiny url.com/mr38ezs8.

10. Charles Joseph Hefele, *A History of the Councils of the Church: From the Original Documents*, vol. 3, *A.D. 431 to 451*, trans. and ed. William R. Clark (Edinburgh: T&T Clark, 1883), 161.

11. Karl Shoemaker, *Sanctuary and Crime in the Middle Ages, 400–1500* (New York: Fordham University Press, 2011). I provide a more substantive discussion of Shoemaker's account of the medieval sanctuary tradition in chapter 6.

12. Renny Golden and Michael McConnell, *Sanctuary: The New Underground Railroad* (Maryknoll, NY: Orbis, 1986), 5.

13. Brittny Mejia, "ICE Agents under Investigation after Fleeing Couple Die in Car Crash," *Los Angeles Times*, April 12, 2018, http://tinyurl.com/4z5exm6y.

14. Simone Browne, *Dark Matters: On the Surveillance of Blackness* (Durham, NC: Duke University Press, 2015), 77. I'm grateful to José Romero for telling me to read this book.

15. See chap. 2 in Browne, *Dark Matters*, 63–88.

16. Browne, *Dark Matters*, 70.

17. Browne, *Dark Matters*, 78.

18. Mae M. Ngai, *Impossible Subjects: Illegal Aliens and the Making of Modern America* (Princeton, NJ: Princeton University Press, 2004), 37.

19. Ngai, *Impossible Subjects*, 18.

20. Ngai, *Impossible Subjects*, 18.

21. Ngai, *Impossible Subjects*, 9.

22. Ngai, *Impossible Subjects*, 19.

23. Ngai, *Impossible Subjects*, 22.

24. See Eduardo Bonilla-Silva, *Racism without Racists: Color-Blind Racism and the Persistence of Racial Inequality in America*, 5th ed. (Lanham, MD: Rowman & Littlefield, 2017).

25. Ngai, *Impossible Subjects*, 23.

26. Ngai, *Impossible Subjects*, 25.

27. *Terrance v. Thompson*, 263 U.S. 197 (1923) at 220–21; quoted in Ngai, *Impossible Subjects*, 47.

28. Ngai, *Impossible Subjects*, 237–39, 258–64.

29. Kevin Kenny documents in detail the interconnections of enslavement, Indian removal, and immigration that have informed our US legal framework of citizenship. In other words, he shows "how the existence, abolition, and legacies of slavery shaped immigration policy as it moved from the local to the federal level over the course of the nineteenth century" and "the tangled origins of the national immigration policies we take for granted today." Kenny, *The Problem of Immigration in a Slaveholding Republic: Policing Mobility in the 19th-Century United States* (Oxford: Oxford University Press, 2023), 2.

30. Greg Grandin, *The End of the Myth: From the Frontier to the Border Wall in the Mind of America* (New York: Metropolitan Books, 2019), 148. I am grateful to Jedediah Purdy for passing along this book to me.

31. Grandin, *End of the Myth*, 40, 58, 65, 96, 106, 217, 275.

32. Grandin, *End of the Myth*, 67.

33. Bill Clinton, "1995 State of the Union Address," filmed January 24, 1995, in Washington, DC, *C-Span*, video, 1:29:30, http://tinyurl.com/yunm4tc5. Grandin mentions Clinton's speech: see Grandin, *End of the Myth*, 245.

34. Grandin, *End of the Myth*, 223.

35. Grandin, *End of the Myth*, 257.

36. Vanessa Romo, "El Paso Walmart Shooting Suspect Pleads Not Guilty," *NPR*, October 10, 2019, http://tinyurl.com/5n8tk53m.

37. Romo, "Shooting Suspect Pleads Not Guilty."

38. Tamara Keith, "'Hate Has No Place' in America, Trump Says After El Paso and Dayton Shootings," *NPR*, August 5, 2019, http://tinyurl.com/dh6nu5xy. Despite Trump's condemnation of the mass murder, the president's campaign rhetoric resembled the shooter's post: see, for example, Peter Baker and Michael Shear, "El Paso Shooting Suspect's Manifesto Echoes Trump's Language," *New York Times*, August 4, 2019, http://tinyurl.com/4n3wxxku.

39. For another helpful account of nativism as a driving force within US politics, see Joseph Nevin's chapter titled "The Ideological Roots of the Illegal as Threat and the Boundary as Protector," in his *Operation Gatekeeper and Beyond: The War on 'Illegals' and the Remaking of the U.S.-Mexico Boundary*, 2nd ed. (New York: Routledge, 2010).

40. Gardner C. Taylor, *How Shall They Preach* (Elgin, IL: Progressive Baptist, 1977), 79. Also see McClendon's discussion of Taylor's insight: James Wm. McClendon Jr., *Systematic Theology*, vol. 1, *Ethics*, rev. ed. (Nashville: Abingdon, 2002), 113.

41. Michel Foucault, *Security, Territory, Population: Lectures at the College de France, 1977–1978*, trans. Graham Burchell (New York: Palgrave Macmillan, 2007), 126–27.

42. Foucault, *Security, Territory, Population*, 127. Foucault doesn't

include Ezekiel in his account of the development of the Hebraic tradition of pastoral care, but his exegesis of other biblical texts includes Ezekiel's imagery of the watchman.

CHAPTER 6

1. Executive Order 13768 of January 24, 2017, "Enhancing Public Safety in the Interior of the United States," *Code of Federal Regulations*, title 8 (2017): 8799–803, §5, http://tinyurl.com/mv3wz6jd.

2. See John Morton, Director, US Immigration and Customs Enforcement, "Enforcement Actions at or Focused on Sensitive Locations," 10029.2 (Washington, DC: October 24, 2011), http://tinyurl.com/2pme2u77.

3. US Department of Justice, Criminal Resource Manual, 1907. Title 8, U.S.C. 1324(a) Offenses. https://www.justice.gov/archives/jm/criminal-resource-manual-1907-title-8-usc-1324a-offenses.

4. Yonat Shimron, "Sanctuary Churches Say Fines against Immigrants Meant to Sow Fear," *Religion News Service*, July 3, 2019, http://tinyurl.com/36y399a4.

5. Elizabeth Dias, "Ordered Deported, Then Sent a $497,777 Fine from ICE," *New York Times*, July 4, 2019, http://tinyurl.com/2jb5dkvy.

6. Yonat Shimron, "ICE Drops $300,000 Fine for an Immigrant in Church Sanctuary," *Religion News Service*, October 25, 2019, http://tinyurl.com/bdhv3rp3.

7. Augustine of Hippo, *The City of God*, 1.1; quoted in Karl Shoemaker, *Sanctuary and Crime in the Middle Ages, 400–1500* (New York: Fordham University Press, 2011), 17.

8. Paulus Orosius, *Histories against the Pagans*, 7.39; quoted in Shoemaker, *Sanctuary*, 17.

9. Shoemaker, *Sanctuary*, 18.

10. Shoemaker, *Sanctuary*, 18.

11. Charles Joseph Hefele, *A History of the Councils of the Church: From the Original Documents*, vol. 3, *A.D. 431 to 451*, trans. and ed. William R. Clark (Edinburgh: T&T Clark, 1883), 161.

12. Shoemaker, *Sanctuary*, 39.

13. Shoemaker, *Sanctuary*, 156.

14. For a helpful account of this era of US military involvement in Central America, see part 1 of Christian Smith, *Resisting Reagan: The U.S. Central America Peace Movement* (Chicago: University of Chicago Press, 1996).

15. Renny Golden and Michael McConnell, *Sanctuary: The New Underground Railroad* (Maryknoll, NY: Orbis, 1986), 5.

16. Hilary Cunningham, *God and Caesar at the Rio Grande: Sanctuary and the Politics of Religion* (Minneapolis: University of Minnesota Press, 1995), xiii.

17. For a theological account of the witness of Óscar Romero's life and ministry, see Edgardo Colón-Emeric, *Óscar Romero's Theological Vision: Liberation and the Transfiguration of the Poor* (Notre Dame, IN: University of Notre Dame Press, 2018).

18. See chap. 2, Robert Tomsho, "Places of Refuge, Acts of Defiance," in *The American Sanctuary Movement* (Austin: Texas Monthly, 1987).

19. Golden and McConnell, *New Underground Railroad*, 48.

20. Golden and McConnell, *New Underground Railroad*, 48.

21. Golden and McConnell, *New Underground Railroad*, 54.

22. For other theological accounts of the significance of ecclesial sanctuary, see Stanley Hauerwas, "A Sanctuary Politics: Being the Church in the Time of Trump," with Jonathan Tran, chap. 8 in *Minding the Web: Making Theological Connections*, with Robert J. Dean (Eugene, OR: Cascade, 2018); and Luke Bretherton, "National: Christian Cosmopolitanism, Refugees, and the Politics of Proxim-

ity," chap. 3 of *Christianity & Contemporary Politics: The Conditions and Possibilities of Faithful Witness* (Oxford: Wiley-Blackwell, 2010).

23. Dave Eggers, "No One Is Safer. No One Is Served," *New Yorker*, August 24, 2018, http://tinyurl.com/y74pp7vm.

24. Eggers, "No One Is Safer."

25. Justin Nortey, "Most White Americans Who Regularly Attend Worship Services Voted for Trump in 2020," Pew Research Center, August 30, 2021, https://tinyurl.com/mryfdahj.

26. Yonat Shimron, "Honduran Woman Who Sought Sanctuary in a Church Will Not Be Deported," *Christian Century*, March 9, 2020, http://tinyurl.com/58bbdphr; see also Sheldon C. Good, "Court Withdraws Deportation Order for Woman in Sanctuary in North Carolina," *Mennonite*, March 2, 2020, http://tinyurl.com/zj3rx8v8.

27. Yonat Shimron, "Federal Court Protects Woman Who Took Sanctuary in a Church from Deportation," *Religion News Service*, February 28, 2020, http://tinyurl.com/mp6ze9vh.

28. Shimron, "Woman Who Took Sanctuary."

29. *Ortez-Cruz v. Barr*, No. 18-1439, 2020 US App. (4th Cir. 2020), at *19. http://tinyurl.com/3k5r8m4z.

30. *Ortez-Cruz*, at *18.

31. *Ortez-Cruz*, at *20.

32. Stanley Hauerwas, *The Peaceable Kingdom: A Primer in Christian Ethics* (Notre Dame, IN: University of Notre Dame Press, 1983), 99.

33. Hauerwas, *Peaceable Kingdom*, 99.

CHAPTER 7

1. Mike Davis, *City of Quartz: Excavating the Future in Los Angeles* (London: Verso, 2006), 122–23.

2. "Elephant with a Headache: Los Angeles and the Poulson Administration," *Frontier* (September, 1955), quoted in Eric Avila, *Popular Culture in the Age of White Flight: Fear and Fantasy in Suburban Los Angeles* (Berkeley: University of California Press, 2006), 157.

3. Nahum M. Sarna, *Understanding Genesis: The World of the Bible in the Light of History* (New York: Schocken Books, 1966), 225.

4. Donald J. Trump (@realDonaldTrump), "We cannot allow all of these people to invade our Country. When somebody comes in, we must immediately, with no Judges or Court Cases," X (formerly Twitter), June 24, 2018, 10:02 a.m., http://tinyurl.com/y4emdb9z.

5. Jeff Sessions, "Attorney General Sessions Delivers Remarks to the Association of State Criminal Investigative Agencies 2018 Spring Conference," March 7, 2018 (Scottsdale, AZ), https://tinyurl.com/yc7f7bc2.

6. Gloria E. Anzaldúa, *The Gloria Anzaldúa Reader*, ed. Ana-Louise Keating (Durham, NC: Duke University Press, 2009), 50.

7. Muricio Rodrígues Ponz, Patricial Vélez Santiago, and Andrea Zárate, "Nos decían ilegales y ahora somos esenciales," *Univision*, June 3, 2020, http://tinyurl.com/2f4ddwdp.

8. Truman Moore, *The Slaves We Rent* (New York: Random House, 1965), x.

9. Moore, *Slaves We Rent*, xi.

10. Harsha Walia, *Undoing Border Imperialism* (Chico, CA: AK Press, 2013), 71.

11. Kelly Lytle Hernández, *Migra! A History of the U.S. Border Patrol* (Berkeley: University of California Press, 2010), 222.

12. Fredric Jameson, *Postmodernism, or the Cultural Logic of Late Capitalism* (Durham, NC: Duke University Press, 1991), xii, xix.

13. Walter D. Mignolo, *The Darker Side of Western Modernity: Global Futures, Decolonial Options* (Durham, NC: Duke University Press, 2011), 8.

14. Aníbal Quijano, "Coloniality of Power, Eurocentrism, and Latin America," in *Coloniality at Large: Latin America and the Postcolonial Debate*, ed. Mabel Moraña, Enrique Dussel, and Carlos A. Jáuregui (Durham, NC: Duke University Press, 2008), 181–224.

15. Eduardo Galeano, *Open Veins of Latin America: Five Centuries of the Pillage of a Continent*, trans. Cedric Belfrage (New York: Monthly Review, 1997 [1973]), 2.

16. Galeano, *Open Veins of Latin America*, 8.

17. Quobna Ottobah Cugoano, *Thoughts and Sentiments on the Evil and Wicked Traffic of the Slavery and Commerce of the Human Species* (1787), in *Unchained Voices: An Anthology of Black Authors in the English-Speaking World of the Eighteenth Century*, ed. Vincent Carretta (Lexington: University Press of Kentucky, 1996), 161.

18. Cugoano, *Thoughts and Sentiments*, 160.

19. Cugoano, *Thoughts and Sentiments*, 165.

20. Cugoano, *Thoughts and Sentiments*, 165–66.

21. Cugoano, *Thoughts and Sentiments*, 166.

22. Cugoano, *Thoughts and Sentiments*, 164.

23. Galeano, *Open Veins of Latin America*, 2.

24. "Another version of what happened between 1500 and 2000 is that the great transformation of the sixteenth century—in the Atlantic that connected European initiatives, enslaved Africans, dismantled civilizations (Tawantinsuyu and Anáhuac, and the already in-decay Maya), and encompassed the genocide in Ayiti (which Columbus baptized Hispaniola in 1492)—was the emergence of a structure of control and management of authority, economy, subjectivity, gender and sexual norms and relations that were driven by Western (Atlantic) Europeans (Iberian Peninsula, Holland, France, and England) both in their internal conflicts and in their exploitation of labor and expropriation of land." Mignolo, *Darker Side of Western Modernity*, 7. I'm indebted to Mignolo for drawing my attention to the life of Ottobah Cugoano.

25. Cugoano, *Thoughts and Sentiments*, 167.

26. Angela Y. Davis, *Freedom Is a Constant Struggle: Ferguson, Palestine, and the Foundations of a Movement* (Chicago: Haymarket, 2016), 107. In her essay entitled "Race and Criminalization," Davis makes clear the inseparability of racism and economics, which produces incarceration as a tool to control populations: "Racism is more deeply embedded in socioeconomic structures, and the vast populations of incarcerated people of color is dramatic evidence of the way racism systematically structures economic relations" (Angela Y. Davis, *The Angela Y. Davis Reader*, edited by Joy James [Oxford: Blackwell, 1998], 66).

27. Gustavo Gutiérrez, *We Drink from Our Own Wells: The Spiritual Journey of a People*, 20th anniversary ed. (Maryknoll, NY: Orbis, 2003), 4.

28. Gutiérrez, *We Drink from Our Own Wells*, 3–4. For Gutiérrez's discussion of the exodus, see 73–75.

29. Gutiérrez, *We Drink from Our Own Wells*, 97.

30. Gutiérrez, *We Drink from Our Own Wells*, 1, 3.

31. Emma Lazarus, *An Epistle to the Hebrews*, centennial edition (New York: Jewish Historical Society of New York, 1987), 30. Fannie Lou Hamer, "Nobody's Free until Everybody's Free" (1971), in *The Speeches of Fannie Lou Hamer: To Tell It Like It Is*, ed. Maegan Parker Brooks and Davis W. Houck (Jackson: University Press of Mississippi, 2011), 134–39.

CONCLUSION

1. Brian Fagan, *The Attacking Ocean: The Past, Present, and Future of Rising Sea Levels* (New York: Bloomsbury, 2013), 226–27.

2. Fagan, *Attacking Ocean*, 226–27.

3. Fagan, *Attacking Ocean*, 236.

4. Fagan, *Attacking Ocean*, 237.

5. Christian Parenti, *Tropic of Chaos: Climate Change and the New Geography of Violence* (New York: Nation, 2012), 9.

6. Parenti, *Tropic of Chaos*, 13.

7. Office of the Director of National Intelligence, *National Intelligence Assessment on the National Security Implications of Global Climate Change to 2030*, Statement for the Record of Dr. Thomas Fingar, Deputy Director of National Intelligence for Analysis, House Permanent Select Committee on Intelligence, June 25, 2008, 16, https://tinyurl.com/2htpt9zc, as quoted in Parenti, *Tropic of Chaos*, 13.

8. *National Intelligence Assessment*, 16, as quoted in Parenti, *Tropic of Chaos*, 13.

9. Parenti, *Tropic of Chaos*, 15.

10. Parenti, *Tropic of Chaos*, 18.

11. Parenti, *Tropic of Chaos*, 11.

12. Parenti, *Tropic of Chaos*, 226.

13. Maria Cristina Garcia, *State of Disaster: The Failure of U.S. Migration Policy in an Age of Climate Change* (Chapel Hill: University of North Carolina Press, 2022), 142.

14. Garcia, *State of Disaster*, 143.

15. Daniel Villafuerte Solís and María del Carmen García Aguilar, "La política antimigrante de Barack Obama y el programa Frontera Sur: Consecuencias para la migración centroamericana," *Migración y desarrollo* (Zacatecas, Mexico) 15, no. 28 (June 2017): 39-64.

16. Fernanda Martínez Flores, "The Effects of Enhanced Enforcement at Mexico's Southern Border: Evidence from Central American Deportees," *Demography* 57, no. 5 (October 2020): 1597-623.

SELECTED BIBLIOGRAPHY

Anzaldúa, Gloria E. *The Gloria Anzaldúa Reader*. Edited by Ana-Louise Keating. Durham, NC: Duke University Press, 2009.

Arriaga, Felicia. *Behind Crimmigration: ICE, Law Enforcement, and Resistance in America*. Chapel Hill: University of North Carolina Press, 2023.

Avila, Eric. *Popular Culture in the Age of White Flight: Fear and Fantasy in Suburban Los Angeles*. Berkeley: University of California Press, 2006.

Barth, Karl. *Church Dogmatics*. 4 vols. Translated by G. W. Bromiley. Edinburgh: T&T Clark, 1956–1975.

———. *Karl Barth and Radical Politics*. 2nd ed. Edited by George Hunsinger. Eugene, OR: Cascade, 2017.

Bonilla-Silva, Eduardo. *Racism without Racists: Color-Blind Racism and the Persistence of Racial Inequality in America*. 5th ed. Lanham, MD: Rowman & Littlefield, 2017.

Bretherton, Luke. *Christianity & Contemporary Politics: The Conditions and Possibilities of Faithful Witness*. Oxford: Wiley-Blackwell, 2010.

Browne, Simone. *Dark Matters: On the Surveillance of Blackness.* Durham, NC: Duke University Press, 2015.

Cantú, Francisco. *The Line Becomes a River: Dispatches from the Border.* New York: Riverhead Books, 2018.

Carretta, Vincent, ed. *Unchained Voices: An Anthology of Black Authors in the English-Speaking World of the Eighteenth Century.* Lexington: University Press of Kentucky, 1996.

Carty, Victoria, and Rafael Luévano, eds. *Mobilizing Public Sociology: Scholars, Activists, and Latin@ Migrants Converse on Common Ground.* Boston: Brill, 2017.

Casa del Migrante, Tecún Umán, ed. *Una luz en el camino: oraciones, salmos, cánticos y una guía para migrantes y peregrinos.* Antigua Guatemala: Copia Fiel, 2013.

Churches in the Believers Church Tradition. *Hymnal: A Worship Book.* Scottdale, PA: Mennonite Publishing House, 1992.

Cohen, Elizabeth F. *Illegal: How America's Lawless Immigration Regime Threatens Us All.* New York: Basic Books, 2020.

Cunningham, Hilary. *God and Caesar at the Rio Grande: Sanctuary and the Politics of Religion.* Minneapolis: University of Minnesota Press, 1995.

Davis, Angela Y. *The Angela Y. Davis Reader.* Edited by Joy James. Oxford: Blackwell, 1998.

———. *Freedom Is a Constant Struggle: Ferguson, Palestine, and the Foundations of a Movement.* Chicago: Haymarket, 2016.

Davis, Ellen F. *Opening Israel's Scriptures.* New York: Oxford University Press, 2019.

Davis, Mike. *City of Quartz: Excavating the Future in Los Angeles.* London, UK: Verso, 2006.

Eggers, Dave. "No One Is Safer. No One Is Served." *New Yorker,* August 24, 2018. http://tinyurl.com/y74pp7vm.

Ellacuría, Ignacio. *Conversión de la Iglesia al Reino de Dios para anun-*

ciarlo y realizarlo en la historia. San Salvador, El Salvador: UCA Editores, 1985.

———. *Ignacio Ellacuría: Essays on History, Liberation, and Salvation.* Edited by Michael E. Lee. Maryknoll, NY: Orbis, 2013.

Eshel, Havah. "Tisha B'Av." *The Reconstructionist* 51, no. 8 (July-August 1986): 7.

Fagan, Brian. *The Attacking Ocean: The Past, Present, and Future of Rising Sea Levels.* New York: Bloomsbury, 2013.

Flores, Fernanda Martínez. "The Effects of Enhanced Enforcement at Mexico's Southern Border: Evidence from Central American Deportees." *Demography* 57, no. 5 (October 2020): 1597–623.

Foucault, Michel. *Security, Territory, Population: Lectures at the College de France, 1977-1978.* Translated by Graham Burchell. New York: Palgrave Macmillan, 2007.

Galeano, Eduardo. *Open Veins of Latin America: Five Centuries of the Pillage of a Continent.* Translated by Cedric Belfrage. New York: Monthly Review, 1997.

Garcia, Maria Cristina. *State of Disaster: The Failure of U.S. Migration Policy in an Age of Climate Change.* Chapel Hill: University of North Carolina Press, 2022.

Golden, Renny, and Michael McConnell. *Sanctuary: The New Underground Railroad.* Maryknoll, NY: Orbis, 1986.

Grandin, Greg. *The End of the Myth: From the Frontier to the Border Wall in the Mind of America.* New York: Metropolitan Books, 2019.

Groody, Daniel G., and Gioacchino Campese, eds. *A Promised Land, A Perilous Journey: Theological Perspectives on Migration.* Notre Dame, IN: University of Notre Dame Press, 2008.

Gutiérrez, Gustavo. *We Drink from Our Own Wells: The Spiritual Journey of a People.* 20th anniversary ed. Maryknoll, NY: Orbis, 2003.

Hauerwas, Stanley. *The Peaceable Kingdom: A Primer in Christian Ethics.* Notre Dame, IN: University of Notre Dame Press, 1983.

———. *Minding the Web: Making Theological Connections.* Eugene, OR: Cascade, 2018.

Hernández, Kelly Lytle. "America's Mass Deportation System Is Rooted in Racism." *The Conversation*, February 26, 2017. http://tinyurl.com/3jrx6twv.

———. *Migra! A History of the U.S. Border Patrol.* Berkeley: University of California Press, 2010.

Honig, Bonnie. *Antigone, Interrupted.* Cambridge, UK: Cambridge University Press, 2013.

Isasi-Díaz, Ada María. *En la lucha (In the Struggle): Elaborating a Mujerista Theology.* Minneapolis: Fortress, 2004.

———. *Mujerista Theology: A Theology for the Twenty-First Century.* Maryknoll, NY: Orbis, 1996.

Jameson, Fredric. *Postmodernism, or the Cultural Logic of Late Capitalism.* Durham, NC: Duke University Press, 1991.

Kenny, Kevin. *The Problem of Immigration in a Slaveholding Republic: Policing Mobility in the 19th Century United States.* Oxford: Oxford University Press, 2023.

Lucero, José Antonio. "Friction, Conversion, and Contention: Prophetic Politics in the Tohono O'odham Borderlands." *Latin American Research Review* 49 (2014): 168–84.

Marquez, Beatriz Aldana, Guadalupe Marquez-Velarde, John M. Eason, and Linda Aldana. "Pushing Them to the Edge: Suicide in Immigrant Detention Centers as a Product of Organizational Failure." *Social Science & Medicine* 283 (August 2021): 114177. https://doi.org/10.1016/j.socscimed.2021.114177.

McClendon, James Wm., Jr. *Systematic Theology.* Vol. 1, *Ethics.* Rev. ed. Nashville: Abingdon, 2002.

Metz, Johann Baptist. *Faith in History and Society: Toward a Practical Fundamental Theology.* Translated by David Smith. New York: Seabury, 1980.

Mignolo, Walter D. *The Darker Side of Western Modernity: Global Futures, Decolonial Options.* Durham, NC: Duke University Press, 2011.

Moore, Truman. *The Slaves We Rent.* New York: Random House, 1965.

Moraña, Mabel, Enrique Dussel, and Carlos A. Jáuregui, eds. *Coloniality at Large: Latin America and the Postcolonial Debate.* Durham, NC: Duke University Press, 2008.

Morrill, Bruce T. *Anamnesis as Dangerous Memory: Political and Liturgical Theology in Dialogue.* Collegeville, MN: Liturgical Press, 2000.

Nevins, Joseph. *Operation Gatekeeper and Beyond: The War on 'Illegals' and the Remaking of the U.S.-Mexico Boundary.* 2nd ed. New York: Routledge, 2010.

Ngai, Mae M. *Impossible Subjects: Illegal Aliens and the Making of Modern America.* Princeton, NJ: Princeton University Press, 2004.

Nguyen, Mai Thi, and Hannah Gill. *The 287(g) Program: The Costs and Consequences of Local Immigration Enforcement in North Carolina Communities.* The Latino Migration Project at The University of North Carolina at Chapel Hill. Chapel Hill: University of North Carolina at Chapel Hill, 2010), v: http://tinyurl.com/3ta84cwh.

Nussbaum, Martha. *The Fragility of Goodness: Luck and Ethics in Greek Tragedy and Philosophy.* 2nd ed. New York: Cambridge University Press, 2001.

Parenti, Christian. *Tropic of Chaos: Climate Change and the New Geography of Violence.* New York: Nation, 2012.

Patterson, Orlando. *Slavery and Social Death: A Comparative Study.* 2nd ed. Cambridge, MA: Harvard University Press, 2018.

Sarna, Nahum M. *Understanding Genesis: The World of the Bible in the Light of History.* New York: Schocken Books, 1966.

Saunders, Frances Stonor. "Where on Earth Are You?" *London Review of Books* 38, no. 5 (March 3, 2016). http://tinyurl.com/bdh32vkw.

Schwartz, Mattathias. "The Anchor." *New Yorker*, April 21, 2014. http://tinyurl.com/2t49cvb5.

Sheridan, Thomas E., and Randall H. McGuire, eds. *The Border and Its Bodies: The Embodiment of Risk Along the U.S.-México Line.* Tucson: University of Arizona Press, 2019.

Shoemaker, Karl. *Sanctuary and Crime in the Middle Ages, 400–1500.* New York: Fordham University Press, 2011.

Smith, Caleb. *The Prison and the American Imagination.* New Haven, CT: Yale University Press, 2009.

Smith, Christian. *Resisting Reagan: The U.S. Central America Peace Movement.* Chicago: University of Chicago Press, 1996.

Sobrino, Jon. *Jesus the Liberator: A Historical-Theological Reading of Jesus of Nazareth.* Maryknoll, NY: Orbis, 1993.

Solís, Daniel Villafuerte, and María del Carmen García Aguilar. "La política antimigrante de Barack Obama y el Programa Frontera Sur: Consecuencias para la migración centroamericana." *Migración y desarrollo* (Zacatecas, Mexico) 15, no. 28 (June 2017): 39–64.

Sölle, Dorothee. *The Mystery of Death.* Minneapolis: Fortress, 2007.

Sophocles. *The Three Theban Plays: Antigone, Oedipus the King, Oedipus at Colonus.* Translated by Robert Fagles. New York: Penguin, 1984.

Stevens, Jacqueline. "America's Secret ICE Castles." *Nation*, December 16, 2009. http://tinyurl.com/3dzhkuse.

Stewart-Sykes, Alistair. *The* Didascalia Apostolorum: *An English Version with Introduction and Annotation.* Turnhout: Brepols, 2009.

Taylor, Gardner C. *How Shall They Preach.* Elgin, IL: Progressive Baptist, 1977.

Timpane, Pilar. "After Samuel Oliver-Bruno's Deportation, a Sanctuary Community Suffers Together." *Sojourners Magazine,* December 3, 2018. http://tinyurl.com/3ctw6y8d.

Tomsho, Robert. *The American Sanctuary Movement.* Austin: Texas Monthly Press, 1987.

Valentín, Benjamín, ed. *In Our Own Voices: Latino/a Renditions of Theology.* Maryknoll, NY: Orbis, 2010.

Wainwright, Geoffrey. *Eucharist and Eschatology.* New York: Oxford University Press, 1981.

Walia, Harsha. *Undoing Border Imperialism.* Chico, CA: AK Press, 2013.

Yoeman, Barry. "ICE Puts Immigrants into a Cruel Catch-22." *Nation,* December 6, 2018. http://tinyurl.com/ycxc52y8.

INDEX